Apocalypse Now and Then

Reading Revelation Today

Paul Barnett

AQUILA
PRESS

A book by Aquila Press

First published November 1989
Reprinted 1992, 1997, 2001
Copyright © Paul Barnett 1989

Aquila Press
PO Box A287, Sydney South, NSW 1235

National Library of Australia
ISBN 1 875861 41 6

Design and cover art by Helen Semmler

Printed in Australia by Southwood Press Pty Limited

CONTENTS

For Anita, my wife

Reading Revelation today 1

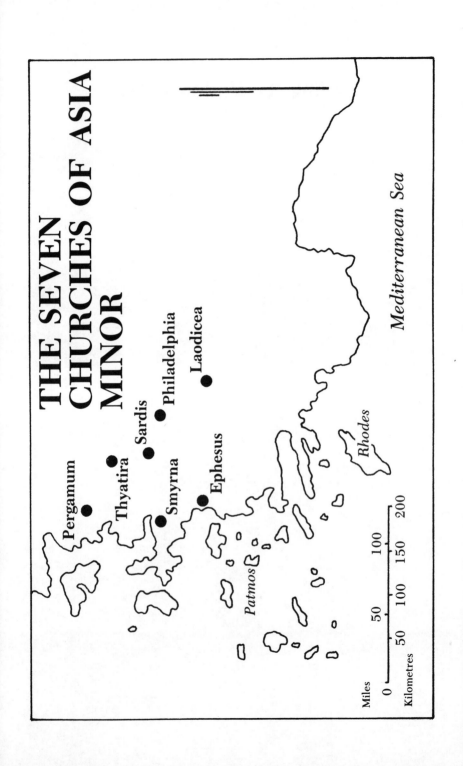

THE SEVEN
CHURCHES OF ASIA
MINOR

Pergamum

Thyatira

Sardis

Smyrna

Philadelphia

Ephesus

Laodicea

Patmos

Rhodes

Mediterranean Sea

Miles

0   50   100   150   200

Kilometres

50   100   150   200

1

Who should read this book?

It is written for ordinary people, who have been intimidated to date by the difficulties in the Book of Revelation.

It could be read as family devotions around the dinner table with the questions at the end of each section used as discussion starters.

But it's also been designed for church use. Preachers should get some help from it, because it came into existence first of all as a series of sermons and bible studies. The study questions at the end of each chapter could be used by a bible-study group in conjunction with a sermon series.

The books of the Bible are really quite short, yet the commentaries are often hundreds of pages long, many times larger than the original work.

The big commentaries have their place. Technical discussion is often needed about the meaning of words, the construction of sentences and what other scholars have written. But the mega-commentaries are not the kind of thing you would read straight through. They are for reference purposes.

This is a mini-commentary. It runs alongside the text of Revelation and keeps the reader in touch with it. It is really trying to highlight the major message as originally written by John while at the same time applying that message to our situation today.

This book will not deal with the technical problems. For that you will need the larger commentaries (for example, by Leon Morris, George Ladd or Robert Mounce). If you would like introductory reading in greater detail, you might like to refer to Donald Guthrie's, *The Relevance of John's Apocalyptic*, (Eerdmans/Paternoster, 1987).

There are nine brief introductory chapters before we commence work on John's text. It would be helpful to read these first, as they will remove many of the reader's difficulties. You should probably refer back to them from time to time.

The *New International Version* is the translation used in this commentary. Words from the NIV are printed in italics.

2

The problem

For most people the last book of the Bible is just too difficult to take seriously. Certainly there are some purple patches like "behold I stand at the door and knock" and the "hallelujah chorus". But much of the rest is considered bizarre, weird and meaningless.

The result is that the book is little read by individuals or preached on in church, apart from the Seven Letters in chapters two and three. Only on rare occasions are passages set down for reading in public worship. Few lectures are given on this book to ministers in training (at least to this minister!) with examination questions only rarely set. It could be said that the Book of the Revelation is one of the most neglected books in the New Testament.

But it is not neglected by all. For some the Revelation is the book above all books of the Bible. It becomes for these people a preoccupation, an obsession. This, however, has not really helped the Revelation; quite the reverse. Those who focus exclusively on this book often appear to hold outlandish views about the Christian faith, at least so it appears to mainstream Christians. If a strange book produces strange Christians, some say leave it to them!

The problem of the Book of the Revelation is not new. Greek speaking Christians in the early centuries associated it with a dangerous breakaway movement called Montanism. Its founder Montanus, who lived early in the second century, came from Phrygia which was quite close to the region of the Seven Churches. It is believed that Montanism may have arisen in some of the churches addressed by John and spread from there soon afterwards into nearby Phrygia.

Certainly there are points of contact between the Revelation and Montanus. Montanists believed that prophets went into trances, that Christ would rule on earth for one thousand years and that the New Jerusalem would descend, quite literally, on Pepuza the city in Phrygia in which Montanism originated. These ideas appear to have arisen from the Book of Revelation. In the following centuries Greek theologians like Dionysius and Eusebius appear to have blamed the Revelation for the evil influence of Montanism, at least in part. They were convinced that their favourite apostle, John, could not have been the author. The John of the Revelation must have been someone else of the same name, whose precise identity was not known. Because of its associations with Montanism this book had some difficulty being accepted within the canon of recognised New Testament books.

Closer to our own times the Revelation has been used extensively by Christian sects and fringe denominations. These groups point to various world crises, especially in the Middle East, as signs of the times heralding the Millennium and Armageddon. American author Hal Lindsey wrote a best-seller about the Revelation with the lurid title *The Late Great Planet Earth*. Even the innocuous triple *b* on an Australian credit card has been unmasked as the the mysterious and evil 666 number referred to in chapter 13!

These bizarre associations along with the sheer difficulty of understanding the text have combined to dampen the interest of many people, both inside and outside the church.

Nonetheless, as we will show, the Revelation has a magnificent and relevant message. It is not nearly so difficult to understand as we might at first think, provided we have the keys to its interpretation.

3

Four keys to Revelation

There are four keys, in particular, which unlock the doors for our understanding of the Revelation. If you take the trouble to read this section, the whole book will immediately begin to make sense. Certainly some things were probably known only to John the author and his original readers and will forever remain obscure. However, it is my belief that with our keys in hand, most of the book will become open to us.

(i) Crack the code

It is quite obvious that what John wrote was "coded" and that it must be deciphered before it can be understood. As to why he wrote so enigmatically we can only speculate. Is it because the *sea beast* and the *harlot* refer to Roman government and he uses veiled language to avoid the charge of treason? Or is it because the transition from history into eternity, which is the subject of his book, is so profoundly inexplicable that he is driven to use symbols, because prosaic statements would simply fail to catch the majesty of the final vision? Possibly both options are true.

Thus the colour *white* and the images of the *throne* and the *crown* each portray conquest and kingly rule.

If *seven* represents God and eternity then *six* probably stands for Satan's pretentious claim to divinity. *Three and a half* or *forty two months*, which is half of seven [years], points to a period within human history which will come to its end . . . unlike God's eternity. *Twelve* and its multiples *twenty four* and *one hundred forty four thousand* relate to God's redeeming of a people: remember the twelve tribes and the twelve apostles? *Ten* is merely a round figure and its multiple *one thousand* represents a great number or a very long period.

In regard to the living creatures, the *lion* represents nobility, the *ox* strength, the *eagle* speed and *mankind* wisdom. The *lamb* probably stands for helplessness.

The *horn* stands for power, the *eye* for knowledge and the *right hand* for authority.

As we begin to read this book and decipher its symbols it becomes clear that the author is a great teacher and pastor. Like the Lord whom he faithfully served, however, John gives his teachings not in wordy abstractions, but in pictures painted from a stock of images of colours, numbers, animals, precious stones, crowns, robes and parts of the body. Our task as readers is to think what these various symbols mean in each episode as it comes before us. These symbols each stand for something and that will become clear as we study each in its context. The one thing we may not do is to take the symbol literally. Classic examples of unhelpful literalism are the 144,000 in chapter 14 and the one thousand year reign of Jesus found in chapter 20. Literalistic use of John's symbolism is quite alien to his intention and has probably done great damage in giving his book a reputation for eccentricity which it has not deserved. These symbols are also listed briefly in the appendix.

(ii) Learn the layout

Our second key to understanding its mysteries is to note that the Revelation is perhaps the most carefully structured book in the New Testament.

While it is called a "book" on several occasions (see 22:6–18) it is in fact written as a letter – a very long letter — which was brought by courier and read aloud in the seven churches in turn (see 1:3–4). The whole book is a letter which contains within it seven short letters. John must have felt that each church needed to hear Christ's message to the other six churches.

Moreover, this "letter-book" describes two visions which John had on the island of Patmos. The first, described in chapter one, relates to the grim condition of the churches in the seven cities of Roman Asia. The letters to the seven churches arise out of this vision. The second vision occurs in chapter four; the remainder of the book is devoted to this second vision.

The second vision relates to the awesome journey God's people must make (chapters 4–20) before the New Jerusalem descends on them (chapters 21–22). After entering the now-opened door into heaven and seeing the majesty of the Enthroned One and the Lamb with the death-wound John traverses the four episodes which are to be the destiny of believers within history.

Each episode contains seven elements, indicating its divine God-ordained character. After the sixth element there is, in each case, an interlude. The seventh then becomes a bridge leading into the new set of seven.

The first episode describes tyranny (6–7), the second chaos in creation (8–11), the third persecution of believers (12–14) and the fourth the destruction of the earth (15–16).

It is here that many have seriously misinterpreted these episodes by imagining them to be end-on-end, a straight line projection of history in advance. On this understanding the reader will be forever trying to calculate, for example, the location in Revelation of World War II, or the Yom Kippur War of 1967.

I believe, however, that these episodes do not follow one another, end-on-end, but rather that they overlap. This means that the tyranny, the chaos, the persecution and the destruction of which we read in these cycles of seven occur right through the historic period (symbolically "one thousand years", the Millennium) which separates Christ's resurrection from his return. These are four strands which together, from John's point of view, make up human history through which God's people must live. He has teased them apart and looked at them in turn. But they are his God-given, prophetic insight into the same historical span. We may set this out as a simple diagram.

Human history: "One thousand years"

6–7   Seven seals depicting TYRANNY

8–11   Seven trumpets depicting CHAOS

12–14   Seven signs depicting PERSECUTION

15–16   Seven plagues depicting DESTRUCTION

Once we understand the layout of the Revelation, that its episodes are concurrent rather than consecutive, many of our difficulties disappear.

(iii) Centre on Christ

It is commonly believed that the thrust of the message of the Revelation lies in the future, in the last great battle

9

between God and his enemies, in the coming cataclysm called Armageddon. If this were the case the Revelation would resemble much of the Jewish literature from that period. The Qumran War Scroll, for example, describes the climactic, end-time battle between the Sons of Light and the Sons of Darkness. Many Christians believe that the basic orientation of the Revelation is like this, focused on a great future battle.

But this is to misread the Revelation in a most fundamental way. It could even be said that the message of this book would remain permanently closed to those who see its perspectives as primarily futuristic. This is a bold statement for which three justifying comments may be made.

First, despite popular belief that Armageddon is a major topic in this book, the fact is that it is only mentioned once in passing (16:16) and with no more significance than other minor references scattered throughout the Revelation. It is not the popularly conceived this-worldly apocalyptic prelude to the Millennium so much as just one of the symbols for the Second Coming of Jesus, or as John calls it, "the great day of God the Almighty" (16:14). It is true that on that occasion "the kings of the whole world . . . assemble . . . for battle". Nonetheless there is no actual battle, merely the language of battle which is used to provide the setting for so momentous an event as the return of Jesus.

Second, there is no actual description of the return of Christ in this book. The promise and the hope of his coming is there (eg 1:7;3:11;16:15;22:7;12,17,20) but no detail is given concerning how or when it will happen. This is curious since there is so much written about the accompanying events like the destruction of the harlot, the beast, the false prophet, and the dragon followed by the great judgment and the coming of the new heaven and earth. The return of Jesus on which these things depend is not even mentioned in chapters 17–21.

Third, and most important, is the great emphasis of the Revelation on the already-completed victory of Jesus. The Revelation leaves us in no doubt: the great end-time battle of God does not lie in the future, but in the past. The battle has been fought and won; Jesus is 'the' blood-stained Victor. This is made clear by some quotations from the book which use the past tense and indicate an action which is completed:

He who conquers I will grant him to sit on my throne as I myself *conquered* and *sat* down with my father on his throne 3:21

The lion of the tribe of Judah, the root of David *has conquered* 5:5

The kingdom of the world *has become* the kingdom of our Lord and of his Christ 11:15

Christ has conquered the twin evils of guilt and death by his own death and resurrection (Colossians 2:15). As a consequence God's kingdom is now a present reality. In the Revelation, as in other parts of the New Testament, the great end-time battle lies in the past not in the future. It is a battle that has been won, once and for all. This is perhaps the most important key to the mysteries of this book. Without this key the meaning of the Revelation will not be unlocked.

(iv) Perceive the parallelism

From chapters 12 to 22 John engages in an audacious parodying of Roman society. He does this by setting certain elements of Roman society in negative parallel with elements of the gospel, as follows:

11

(a) The imagery of the godly woman — persecuted in chapter 12, the pristine bride of Christ in chapter 21 — is paralleled by the "great harlot" in chapter 17.

(b) The New Jerusalem, the Holy City in chapters 21–22 corresponds with but surpasses by far Babylon the Great (= Rome) in chapter 18.

(c) "The Lamb as though slain" (Greek: *hos esphagmenon* 5:6,12;13:8) is paralleled by "the beast from the sea" one of whose heads "seemed to have a mortal wound" (*hos esphagmenen* 13:3). The Beast from the sea is the Roman Emperor, as represented by the Provincial Governor.

(d) The Beast has an image, that is a statue, and those who worship the beast through his image have the mark of his name on their foreheads (13:15–17; 14:9,11; 16:2; 19:20; 20:4). In parallel but by contrast the servants of God worship God and the Lamb and refuse to worship the Beast. They will bear the name of the Lamb on their foreheads (22:3–4).

(e) The community of Christ, the bride of Christ, which is characterised by chastity, truthfulness and endurance (14:4–5), is paralleled by the community of the Beast, the great harlot, characterised by murder, fornication, sorcery and falsehood (21:8; 22:15).

John sees the the sovereignty of God and of the Lamb as being so infinitely higher than the pretentious claims of Caesar that the latter becomes, by contrast, a demonic imitation of the Lord God Almighty and of the One who is the ruler of the kings of the earth. For John the religion of Caesar is the cult of the devil, which grotesquely apes the true worship of God and of the Lamb.

John had good reason to depict Caesar religion in this way. Caesar religion was the faith of the greatest empire in history. Its legions were invincible. It had conquered, colonised and Romanised all the nations that ringed the Mediterranean. Beautiful cities had been erected in every country with a splendid network of military roads between them. In many cities of Roman Asia temples had been built for the veneration of the Emperor's statue. All public occasions were marked by religious acknowledgement of the Emperor. The poets Virgil and Horace declared that with the coming of Augustus a new age had dawned. Many inscriptions spoke of the Emperor as a god and a saviour and that the new age had now come.

One of the keys therefore to open the Revelation is the perception of the parallelism which John has daringly set up and by which he ridicules the political ideology of the Roman State and the outrageous claims it made upon the loyalty of its subjects. As such a prophet John is really a strident critic of Rome. John the prophet of Patmos became for Christians of Asia what the classic prophets of Israel had been centuries before in their denunciations of the nations surrounding Israel.

The most urgent challenge by John to his readers is that they worship God and the redeemer Lamb, not the pseudo and pretentious counterpart, the Roman Emperor, by means of the Imperial cult which had spread rapidly throughout the cities of Roman Asia.

Worship was a test of true conviction and loyalty. To worship Caesar as god was to deny Christ as Lord. To worship God Almighty and the Lamb was to deny Caesar. The many expressions of worship in the Revelation affirm from the heart and with the mouth that God and the Lamb were the only ones to whom one could entrust one's all. Worship is the mind's conviction and the mouth's confession that reality, truth and goodness are to be found in God and the Lamb and not in any other.

This means that for us worship has both a positive and negative aspect. In affirming that truth, salvation and power reside in God is to deny that these are to be found in the many options which constantly present themselves before us. As we live in the world day by day, and as we meet together with fellow-believers our lives are to be characterised by worship. But this demands not only that we say "yes" to God and the Lamb, but also that we say "no" to every false alternative.

4

The gospel in Revelation

Revelation appears to be different from other parts of the New Testament. But is it? In his opening chapter John establishes the threefold character of God. He pronounces grace and peace

from him who is ... who was ... who is to come; from the seven spirits who are before his throne; from Jesus Christ (1:4,5)

Here, as elsewhere in the New Testament, we see the doctrine of the Trinity in embryo. As heresies arose in later centuries the Christian church developed more detailed statements about God's triune character, as for example in the creed formulated at the Council of Nicaea in AD 325. The seminal, threefold outline and content of such creeds, however, is to be found within the New Testament in passages such as this one.

God is spoken of as the majestic Enthroned One whose sovereignty spans history. Thus he is "the beginning and the end", "the alpha and omega" (1:8), he who is, who was and who is to come. He is called the "living God" (7:2), the thrice holy one (4:8), and repeatedly referred to as *pantokrator* (for example, 1:8), all powerful. He is characterised by both "grace" (1:4) and "wrath" (16:1). Not least he is the "father" of Jesus (for example, 1:6). But God is not spoken of as "father" of Christian believers as elsewhere in the New Testament (but see 21:7). Surrounded by his heavenly hosts this king-like God governs history and the universe in all their chaos and rebellion, bringing the nations at the last to acknowledge him in his righteous acts (15:4).

The numerous references to the seven spirits obviously refers to God's Spirit. As mentioned in chapter 3, seven is the divine or eternal number. But there are also some references to *the* Spirit which clearly point to the Spirit of God, the third of the persons in the divine triad. John declares on a number of occasions that he was "in the Spirit" which is taken to mean that he was prophesying as inspired by the Spirit (1:10; 17:3;21:10).

It is to *Jesus Christ*, however, that most attention in this book is directed. God has bestowed the honour of directly ruling history on Jesus, the Son of God. He is "lion of the tribe of Judah, the root of David" come in fulfilment of many Old Testament Promises (for example, Genesis 49:9,10; Isaiah 11:1,10; Jeremiah 23:5;33:15). As God's Messiah or Christ he shares with God the kingdom of the world and over the nations (11:15,18). He is the "ruler of the kings of the earth" (1:5).

This Christ through whom God governs history is spoken of in terms which indicate that John regarded him as a divine figure. He sits with his father on the father's throne (for example, 3:21) and is worshipped as his father is (for example, 5:13). Like his father he is called "alpha and omega, the first and last, the beginning and the end" (22:13). He declares himself to be I AM (1:8; 22:13) in terms reminiscent of Yahweh's great self-disclosure of Exodus 3:14. John's picture of him with hair "white like wool, as white as snow" (1:14) suggests that we must think of Jesus in terms of the "ancient of days" in Daniel's majestic vision of Yahweh (Daniel 7:9).

Nonetheless, this ruler's dominion of history and of the nations does not depend on his deity, which is undoubted, but on his victory in the climactic, end-time battle of God. It is precisely at this point that the Revelation and indeed the New Testament takes us completely by surprise. The victory of God lies not in the future but in the past and that victory occurred, unimaginably, not in a military campaign but in the death of Jesus. The crowning paradox of the gospel is that Jesus is the Lion of Judah, the Christ authorised to exercise his Father's dominion over history, precisely because he is the Lamb who was slain. He is "worthy to take the book and open its seals" because (Greek: *hoti*) he was "slain and purchased men for God by [his] blood"(5:9). The basis of Jesus' Lordship is not his divine status but his redemptive death.

Perhaps the very centre of Revelation's message is found in the words "the Lion of the tribe of Judah . . . has conquered" (5:5). We learn two things from this. First, the aorist tense of the verb *nikan* teaches that it is an already completed victory. Second, the verb's lack of an object indicates that the conquest is absolute and unlimited (so also in 3:21). Mathias Rissi, an American scholar, commented that "for [John] there is only one victory of Christ; it was won in the past and resulted in the debilitation of all enemy powers, once and for all".

In its numerous statements about Jesus it is clear that Revelation's author was attuned to the outlines of the Gospel message as found elsewhere in the New Testament. The following extracts from the Revelation show how closely the author followed the evangelical proclamation as set out in other parts of the Apostolic writings.

17

2:18	. . . the Son of God . . .	cf Rom 1:3,4
5:5	. . . the root of David	Rom 1:3
1:5	. . . who loves us . . . has freed us from our	
	sins by his blood	Gal 2:20
1:5	. . . the firstborn from the dead	1 Cor 15:4
12:5	. . . caught up to God	Acts 1:2
1:5	. . . the ruler of the kings of the earth	1 Cor
		15:25
1:7	. . . he is coming with the clouds	1 Thess 3:17

Clearly John understands and is committed to declaring the gospel of Jesus. It was on account of "the word of God and the testimony of Jesus" that he was in exile on lonely Patmos. Graeme Goldsworthy in his aptly titled book *Gospel in Revelation* (Paternoster, 1984) has shown how *evangelical* a work the Revelation is and that it is not, as is often implied, the "odd one out" in the New Testament. Jesus, Son of God, long-expected messiah from the line of David, motivated by love died redemptively for sins, was raised from the dead, caught up to God as ruler of history and will return in triumph to herald the judgment of God and the consummation of the ages. The gospel is, therefore, as central in this book as in any other within the canonical scriptures. Its form is unusual but its essential message is the same.

In placing the emphasis it does on the gospel, the Revelation rather surprisingly says next to nothing about the life of Jesus. Apart from the one reference to the male child menaced by the dragon in chapter 12 (Herod in Matthew 2?) the Revelation focuses our attention on Jesus' death, resurrection, ascension, rule and return. The emphasis in this book is similar to what Peter and Paul write in their letters and what they say in their speeches in the Acts of the Apostles. This is rather different from the Gospels where our attention is directed to the things Jesus did and said within the period of his public ministry.

One of the characteristics of the Revelation is what might be called its two-beat rhythm. Have you noticed how frequently expressions of worship are offered to the enthroned one or to the lamb? But these are regularly in response to gospel-statements. The first beat of the rhythm is evangelic and the second is worshipful response. This pattern appears repeatedly within Revelation. For example:

4:8   Holy, holy, holy, is the Lord God Almighty who is and was and is to come.

This evangelical statement, made by the four living creatures, is responded to in worship by the 24 elders who sing

4:11 Worthy art thou, our Lord and God, to receive glory and honour and power, for thou didst create all things . . .

This two beat gospel/worship format occurs repeatedly throughout the entire book.

5

If Christ has conquered, why is there evil?

All that John says about the already-accomplished conquest of Christ raises the obvious question: why then is there evil? If God has taken his great power and begun to reign, why is it that we see and experience the tyranny, chaos, persecution and destruction which the Revelation so graphically depicts? If the kingdom of the world has become the Kingdom of our Lord and of his Messiah why are we surrounded by pain and misery?

The briefest reading of this book leaves us with no romantic illusions about the dark side of human experience within history. No book of the Bible is as candid about evil and suffering as the Revelation of John. The surface of the world is the scene of unfolding horror. From the dark depths beneath it burst forth the terrifying creatures of an evil king which assault humanity (9:1–11). From heaven above is cast down the powerful and great dragon who relentlessly pursues and punishes the people of the Lamb. If the earth is so appalling, then heaven, with which it is constantly contrasted by alternating references, is serene, beautiful, pure and good.

20

So, to return to our question, how are we to reconcile Christ's already-achieved victory with the evil we see on every hand and which this book describes in such frank terms?

There can be no doubt that the Revelation attributes the evil in the world and within history to the Devil.

This malicious persona is variously described. He is a king from the bottomless pit with the names *Abbadon* (Hebrew) and *Apollyon* (Greek), both of which mean "destroyer". His evil creatures torture and kill huge numbers of the human race regardless that they are his people anyway (see Chapter 9). He is as much an enemy to people in general as he is to believers.

Despite this, however, the Revelation repeatedly portrays God as mercifully restraining the destructive powers of this evil king. Thus, while a quarter of mankind is killed in the tyrant's wars in the episode of the horsemen, three quarters are to be spared (6:8). In the episode of the trumpets that follows, a third of the earth, trees, grass, sea, rivers, humans was destroyed; but two thirds are to be spared (chapters 8-9). The devil is permitted by God to bring destruction.

But God is not the source of the evil. Indeed we see God repeatedly acting in mercy to limit and restrain evil. God's limitation of the extent of satanic destruction is specifically to provide rebellious humanity with the opportunity to repent from their worship of demons and idols and from their breaking of God's commandments (9:20). There is a note of deep pathos as the author remarks on several occasions that "they did not repent" of their sins (9:21; 16:9,11) but rather cursed God for the evil that had fallen on them. Yet the truth is that God has restrained the totality of evil that will come in the final judgment precisely to give the nations the opportunity to

21

turn back to him. It is a severe mercy, to be sure, but mercy nonetheless.

The most sustained image of the Devil, however, is that of the great red dragon with seven crowned heads and ten horns. He is called the Devil and Satan and identified as the ancient serpent who appears in Genesis chapter three. He is the great deceiver of the nations of the world who has deluded humanity to believe that God the creator is not to be given his due place (12:9). Additionally he brings great suffering to Christian believers: he accuses them night and day before God (12:10).

The Revelation makes it plain why the dragon brings such pain to Christians. It is because the male child Jesus has been caught up to God (12:5) and, as a consequence, that salvation and the kingdom of God have now come (12:10). This is the reason the dragon has been thrown down to earth where he rages against and assails those who belong to the Lamb (12:10). Christ's already-completed redemptive conquest is the direct cause of the Satan-inspired persecution of Christians of which chapter 13 speaks.

Paradoxically, Revelation also describes the Devil as bound by a chain and kept in a pit, under lock and key (20:1–2). The Devil's imprisonment is for the duration of the one thousand years, a symbolic reference to the historical period separating the "first resurrection" (that is, Christ's resurrection) and the "second death" (that is, hell, in the lake of fire — 21:8). Clearly the one thousand years, or the millennium as it is sometimes called, is that period of time — however long it will actually prove to be — between Christ's resurrection and his return. At the end of the "one thousand years" the dragon will be released for a "little while" (20:3) before being thrown into the lake of fire where he will be tormented forever (20:10).

Thus, on the one hand the dragon is said to be thrown down to the earth to persecute the believers (chapter 12) while on the other hand, he is described as imprisoned awaiting final torments of the lake of fire (chapter 20). The question is: how free is the Devil at this time? Is there any discrepancy between the two versions mentioned above, in which he is free and active in the one but imprisoned in the other?

The answer, found in both chapters, is that those who belong to Jesus share in his conquest. Even though killed they are not defeated since they are now alive and share with Jesus in his "thousand year" rule (20:4–6). They have shared with Christ in his "first resurrection" and can never be subjected to the "second death" which the dragon and the unbelieving nations of the world face. John writes that "they have conquered [the dragon] by the blood of the Lamb and by the word of their testimony, for they loved not their lives even unto death" (12:11).

In both pictures, therefore, the Devil though active on the surface of the world, is restrained and limited by the courageous belief and faithful witness of Christians. The time will come, however, when his activity, limited as it is, will come to an end as he is finally cast into the lake of fire. How are Christians to live in the mean time?

6

Sharing Christ's conquest

In the face of this evil, Christians are continually called on to display patience and faithfulness to Jesus. In the episode relating to persecution (chapters 12–14) John writes grimly:

If any one is to be taken to captivity, to captivity he goes; If any one slays with the sword, with the sword must he be slain.

Here is a call for the endurance and faith of the saints. 13:10.

It is by endurance and faith that believers share in the completed conquest of the Lamb who was slain.

Through Jesus' redemptive death and their fidelity to him believers exercise his rule over the Devil and all his evil forces. These faithful ones rule on earth during their lifetimes and they rule from heaven after their death. John's words indicate that they rule on earth:

Worthy art thou [O Lamb] . . .
thou wast slain and by thy blood didst ransom men for God . . .
and hast made them a kingdom and priests to our God, and they shall reign on earth. 5:9–10 (RSV).

Alternatively their rule may be from heaven. If they have lost their lives on earth in faithful witness they will rule with the Lamb from heaven throughout the "thousand years". Of these John says:

... *I saw the souls of those who had been beheaded for their testimony to Jesus and for the word of God ...*
... they came to life, and reigned with Christ a thousand years ...
Blessed and holy is he who shares in the first resurrection
... they shall be priests of God and of Christ,
and they shall reign with him a thousand years. 20:4–6 (RSV).

Therefore whether alive on earth, or raised from death to life with Christ in heaven, the faithful people of the Lamb are victorious against all the malevolent forces pitted against them. They share his messianic rule as the Lion of the tribe of Judah. But this is because he is the Lamb who was slain. The writer therefore places great emphasis on the importance and the power of faithful witness. Again and again he calls on his readers "to conquer", that is, to remain faithful to Jesus, even though they suffer and die (for example, 2:7,11,17,26).

Those who conquer will inherit all the blessings of the New Jerusalem (21:7).

This then is the conquest, the triumph of Christian believers as set out in the Book of Revelation. It is the humble triumph of patient faith in the face of deadly opposition, a triumph which will be realised in physical terms only at the end, in the New Jerusalem.

Regrettably, in the centuries that followed, when the Church became a powerful institution, a this-worldly triumphalism came to the fore. The emperor Constantine had the first two letters of Christ's name (*Xp*) inscribed on the shields of his soldiers as a means of securing victory in battle. Crusades were fought against the Muslim infidel to save the holy sites in Palestine. Missionary work was done in tandem with the colonialists' sword and gunboat. More recently, church growth has been promoted in what are frankly triumphalist terms. But it is all very remote from the conquest of the Lamb which the Revelation calls its readers to share.

But what were the problems which John's original readers faced? What was it they had to conquer?

7

Three problems facing John's readers

There were three basic problems faced by John and and his readers at that time.

(i) Jewish hostility

The "synagogue of Satan" at Smyrna and Philadelphia (2:9; 3:9) almost certainly refers to the grave problems now created for Christians in these cities by the Jewish synagogues. Although Jews were disliked within the Graeco-Roman cities of the empire, their communities were, in comparison with the churches, both well-established and well-connected. This was particularly the case in Roman Asia. Jewish leaders had a good network of connections within the empire and they had long since come to regard the rapidly growing Christian movement as a schismatic and heretical cult.

Their opposition could only have been intensified by the reversals they had suffered at the hands of the new regime of emperors Vespasian and his sons Titus and Domitian. These emperors were much more severe towards the Jews than the Julio-Claudian dynasty which had preceded them. As military commanders of the

Roman armies in Palestine, Vespasian and Titus had first-hand experience of Jewish fanaticism. Under these leaders Jerusalem had been sacked and the temple destroyed. After the war, in a highly symbolic gesture, Vespasian compelled the international community of Jews to pay a tax, formerly given for the upkeep of the temple of Yahweh their God in Jerusalem, to the temple of the god Jupiter in Rome. But the Christians were not required to pay this tax, which was known as the *fiscus Judaicus*. That Christians were free from this obligation probably intensified the bitterness of the Jews towards them.

Nonetheless, the *fiscus Judaicus* did secure immunity for the Jews from participating in the rituals of the Imperial Cult, an immunity which Christians did not enjoy. The Jewish communities in Smyrna and Philadelphia may have earned the name "synagogue of Satan" because they reported the identity of Christians to the provincial authorities.

(ii) Heretical infiltration

Three of the churches had been infiltrated by various false teachings. The churches of Ephesus and Pergamum were troubled by a group known as the "Nicolaitans". The churches of Pergamum and Thyatira suffered, respectively, from the "teachings of Balaam" and from the influence of a prophetess whom John calls "Jezebel". Doubtless John's readers knew what was intended by these sinister sounding references. We can only guess at their meaning. There is no way of knowing who the "Nicolaitans" were, since nothing else is known about them. The "Teaching of Balaam" which the prophetess "Jezebel" apparently taught, encouraged the eating of idol-sacrificed food and laxity in sexual matters, and gravely undermined the churches in Pergamum and Thyatira.

(iii) Caesar worship

Life for Gentile converts living in the pagan world of that time was always difficult. Fearful that some jealous deity might be offended, a multitude of gods were worshipped in the many temples of the Graeco-Roman world. Bizarre mystery religions from the East promising healing and immortality flourished in the cities and towns of the empire. Anxious for the future, many people consulted astrologers and diviners. Desire to control events and other people led to the widespread practice of magic. Unlike Judaism and Christianity where sexuality was restricted to marriage, the various pagan religions of the time accepted as normal a whole range of sexual practices, including temple prostitution, homosexuality and paedophilia. One has only to read First Corinthians to sense the pressures from a pagan society which were on Christian believers. Jews were required to keep to themselves, so that the pressures did not impinge on them directly. Christians, however, were not discouraged from normal everyday fraternization with unbelievers. They were subject to daily conflict.

The situation for Christians in Asia had worsened. The cult of Caesar worship had its origins in that province. For more than a century temples for Rome and the emperor had been constructed. There is archaeological evidence that Roman governors had increasingly participated in rituals for local deities, with a view to tying these more closely to Rome. A great temple for Domitian had been built in Ephesus, next to which was an eight metre high statue of the emperor. According to Suetonius, the Emperor Domitian had decided that he should be called "Lord and God" (*Domitian* 13). As reports came to John on Patmos, he probably discerned that in a very short time, life for Christians would become very painful indeed. Already Antipas had been killed in Pergamum, "where Satan's throne is" (2:13).

There is a mood of impending crisis running through John's book:

1.3 *The time is short*
2.10 *. . . the devil is about to throw some of you into prison.*
3.10 *. . . the hour of trial is coming on the whole earth.*
12.12 *. . . woe to you O earth . . . the devil has come down to you in great wrath.*

History has proved John's prophecy to have been correct. From the time he wrote and for the next 200 years the Roman state and the Christians were locked in mortal combat. Antipas was but one of thousands to have died as martyrs for Jesus. For periods of several years at a time the Roman state virtually declared war on the church. Only after Constantine emerged victorious at the battle of Milvian Bridge AD 312 was there peace for the Christians.

John's prophecy is correct, however, in a much broader sense. Down to our own time Christians have suffered whenever the state has demanded the allegiance that can only be given to God and the Lamb. One has only to think of the policies in the present century of Stalin and Hitler towards Christians to see that John's prophecy has been confirmed in its accuracy many times over.

8

Who was John?

Although the writer identifies himself only as "John" (1:1,4,9; 22:8) there are good reasons to believe him to have been John Zebedee, the apostle. Christian writers of the second century were in no doubt that the author was John Zebedee. Justin Martyr who wrote only 50 years later and Irenaeus who wrote about 80 years later declared the Revelation to be written by John the apostle.

Second, the writer had extensive knowledge of the cities of Asia in which the churches were located. His "eye salve to anoint your eyes" (3:18) suggests he knew the Laodiceans produced eye salve. He addressed the seven churches by an order which was indicated by the network of roads between them. Clearly this John knew Asia. But so did John Zebedee who according to Irenaeus, lived for many years in Ephesus.

Third, the exile on Patmos had a detailed knowledge about each of the seven churches. He knew their strengths and their weaknesses. He knew of pressures from Jews and the subleties of heretical infiltration. He was aware of the escalating pressures of Caesar worship.

Moreover, he writes not only with great knowledge but also with immense authority. No introduction is needed beyond the name of John. He wrote expecting his words to be heeded in the way we would expect an apostolic author to write.

Fourth, there are many allusions in what John has written to the Gospel and Letters of John. The number seven, as we have seen, is important in the Revelation; there are seven signs in the Gospel of John. Terms like "life", "death", "thirst", "victory", "word", "lamb" and "I AM" sayings occur in both sets of writings, but not elsewhere in the New Testament. The rare word "pierced", in reference to the crucifixion, occurs in the New Testament only in both sets of writings. Consider also, the similarities between the following passages:

Revelation 21:6	John 7:37	John 4:14
to the thirsty I will give from the fountain of the water of life.	If any one thirst let him come to me and drink.	the water I will give him will become a spring of water … to eternal life.

The similarity between the Revelation and two passages in the Gospel of John, which do not occur in any other New Testament author, strongly suggest common authorship of the two sets of literature.

Difference of style between Revelation and the Fourth Gospel was noticed by Christians from the third century onwards, and was offered as evidence that the John of Revelation is not John the Evangelist. However, the similarity between the documents is also striking. Perhaps different scribes assisted John in his work so that the varying styles may be explained along those lines.

9

Other interpretations

The unusual imagery in the Revelation has given rise to differing approaches to its interpretation. The theory of interpretation one takes at the outset tends to dictate the meaning of the book as it unfolds.

Throughout the history of Christianity three main theories have emerged:

(1) Preterist

Taking its name from the Latin *praeter* (past), the preterist view interprets details in the book only in terms of the historical perspectives of the writer, John, and readers. Accordingly the Revelation has no message for any later generation. In effect, the book is of interest only to historians of the ancient past.

Against this theory it must be objected that only a lesser part of Revelation would have been meaningful to John's contemporaries. Had readers of the day been told that the whole message of the book applied to them at that time they would probably have been baffled.

(2) Futurist

At the other extreme the futurist view considers that everything in the book relates to the End of the Age, with special emphasis on Armageddon and the Millennium. The Seven Letters (chapters 2–3) are seven preliminary historical eras or "dispensations", the last of which, the Laodicean, will be characterised by the lukewarmness of the church. The 1000 years (chapter 20) is a literal future period of Christ's reign on earth prior to the Final End. The version of futurism which arose in the early church was called "Chiliasm", after the Greek *chilioi*, a thousand. In modern times it is sometimes called "Dispensationalism".

One difficulty with the futurist theory is that it does not do justice to the critical needs of original Christian readers in Ephesus, Smyrna and the other cities which the writing of the Revelation sought to meet. Another weakness is its failure, on one hand, to understand the symbolic nature of a work written in an apocalyptic style, and on the other, that it takes John's symbols literally.

Furthermore, the futurist view makes Revelation (and the Book of Daniel) the key to unlock the Christian understanding of the "Last Things". Other Christians believe that the proper place to begin to understand the future is with the teaching of Jesus in Mark 13 (and parallel Gospel passages). This is the procedure followed by authors of the New Testament Letters. The Revelation should fit in with Jesus' timetable, followed as it was by the Letters of Paul, Peter and John; not the reverse.

(3) Historicist

According to this view the Revelation is a forecast of the whole of history, from John's time through to the return of Christ. Revelation calls itself "prophecy" and this is taken to mean that, from the standpoint of the author and the readers, the message relates to specific future events.

The weakness of this theory is that only a small part of the book can be relevant at any one time. The book's symbolic presentation means that there can be little agreement on what stage of history has been reached at any one time, or who, for example, is symbolised by Hitler or Stalin. The weakness of the historicist approach may be seen in the lack of consensus about the meaning of historical events among historicist advocates.

It seems that each of the views above is beset by problems. Yet each has one or more insights. The theory of interpretation we adopt in this commentary, but for which we have no single–word title, is marked by the following:

i. It will follow the *preterist* view to the extent that the modern reader's first step will always be to ask what the original readers would have understood the book to have meant. The past is vitally important; we need to know as much as possible about the historical circumstances of John's readers.

ii. It will agree with the *futurist* view that the End is critical to the meaning of the book. The overthrow of God's enemies, the vindication of God's people, the return of Christ, the gathering of God's people unto him, are fundamental to the interpretation of Revelation. Not to notice the emphasis on the future will prevent us understanding the message of Revelation.

iii. It will agree with the *historicist* view in seeing the book as a preview of history, but in the sense of major recurring themes, not necessarily of detailed events. Readers at any point in history should be able to see the Revelation as a God–given commentary on the conflict, persecution and destruction which, in varying degrees, is always occurring . . . including at this present moment of history.

In addition to the above, readers should approach the text with two further things in mind:

a) We should note that Revelation is an expanded treatment of the gospel message of Christ: his death and resurrection, his present Lordship over history as God's Christ, his judgment of God's enemies, cosmic and human and the final reunion of God and his people forever. Revelation is an *evangelical* work.

b) We should understand that the book is couched in its own distinctive *apocalyptic* language, which with a little effort, readers can master. But it must be read in the terms in which the writer gives, not those which the reader brings to the text.

✿   ✿   ✿   ✿   ✿   ✿   ✿   ✿   ✿   ✿   ✿   ✿

The preliminary statements are now completed. We turn to the text of the Revelation. The reader is encouraged to open the New International Version and to read the passage on which commentary is being given.

Reading Revelation today II

10

Patmos 1:1–20

(1)   What John wrote (1:1–8)

John saw two visions. One is referred to in 1:9–20, the other in 4:1. The whole of what John now writes in this "book" (1:11 RSV) arises out of these two visions. These two visions form the substance of what he calls *the revelation* (= unveiling) of *Jesus Christ* (v.1).

This "revelation" originated from God who gave it to [Jesus] who in turn sent *his angel* to his *servant John* (v.2).

Who was this "angel"? I think it was a human messenger from the churches of Asia, who had come to Patmos to tell the revered Christian leader about the grave difficulties Christians were then facing in the mainland cities. As John reflected in "the Spirit" on this news from Asia, God gave him the two visions about which he proceeds to write.

John calls what he writes *the words of this prophecy* (v.3) and says that these *must soon take place* (v.1), *because the time is near* (v.3). Once completed, couriers were to bring the "book" to the seven cities in turn where it was to be read aloud to the assembled congregations. The "book" is in the form of letter (v.4) written to the Christians in Asia. As such it is by far the longest letter within the New Testament.

Clearly John is writing his "prophecy" for the benefit of hearers who were at that time facing suffering and death, which "must soon take place" in the churches in Roman Asia. This is not to say for one moment, however, that John's words only apply to the hearers in the immediate times about which he wrote. His "book" is profoundly applicable to Christians throughout the whole of human history. But as always in reading scripture, we must begin by asking what the writer meant his original readers to understand. Only then can we ask what his words mean for us now.

We may note in passing that John appears to regard what he has written as scripture. Such considerations as his reference to "the prophecy of this book" (22:7,10,18 cf 1:3,11), to a "revelation" which originated with God (1:1), to the fact that it was to be read aloud in the churches (1:3), and that it was not to be added to nor subtracted from (22:18–19) strongly suggest that the author regarded what he had written as "holy scripture".

But is this "book", as it unfolds, a series of predictions, as many believe? Are we intended to see its prophecies as surely fulfilled by the crises and disasters of later generations, including our own generation? The answer is both "no" and "yes". It is not John's intention to give a detailed or event-specific preview of world history, as for example the French astrologer Nostradamus did in the 16th century. Rather, John gives a prophetic interpretation of those evil forces which were and are at work within history before the final return of Jesus as they will affect people in general and Christians in particular. John's prophecy insofar as it relates to the future, however, is not event-specific but general in character.

John is not so much focusing on the future as on the past. The future is entirely controlled by the past. The past in question is, of course, the already-completed victory of Jesus over those evil forces which were against him and which, though defeated, remain to afflict those who bear witness to him. Understood in this way the futuristic references are made in order to identify as demonic the sources of suffering to Christians and others in the world and to show that, in the words of Luther's great hymn, "their doom is writ". Indeed it is. Christ has conquered, prevailed, triumphed; the victory is his, the outcome not in doubt.

It is for this reason that in writing the Revelation John speaks as one who *testifies to everything he saw* (v.3). This he immediately identifies as *the word of God ... the testimony of Jesus.* The words "testify" and "testimony" are first cousins and derive from the well-known New Testament word "witness", a word we associate with declaring the gospel-message about Jesus. In other words, John's "prophecy" is not a series of bizarre forecasts about future historical events but a presentation of the "word of God", that is, the "testimony" or "witness" to Jesus. It is nothing more or less than the gospel of Jesus as applied to the sufferings of believers in a hostile environment. This is brought out clearly in John's important definition offered later: "The testimony of (= about) Jesus is the spirit of Prophecy" (19:10). Put simply, John is saying "evangelism is prophecy".

This view is confirmed by two elements that immediately follow. First, in the formal greeting of this lengthy letter John prays that his readers will enjoy the blessings of *grace* and *peace* (v.4). What is really significant, especially from one who was evidently a Jew and whose credo would have been avowedly monotheistic, is that these twin blessings derive

*from **him** who is and who was and who is to come*
*from **the seven spirits** before his throne*
*from **Jesus Christ*** (vs.4–5).

Whereas to a Jew all blessings would have been invoked in the name of Yahweh, the one, true, living God, the blessings of which John writes flow from a triad. The relationships between the three are not spelt out, but there can be no doubt that an early expression of trinitarian belief is in mind.

The references to God in this work are many. Shortly (in 1:8) the Lord God will declare in self-revelation:

I AM (as in Exodus 3:14)
the Alpha and the Omega (first and last letters in the Greek alphabet, revealing God's Lordship over history)
who is and who was and who is to come (who spans history and eternity),
the Almighty (this word, *pantokrator*, is a title for God which occurs within the Greek Old Testament).

According to the Roman writer Suetonius, Domitian (the Emperor at the time John wrote) demanded that people called him "Lord God" (*Domitian* 13). But the ruler of the world and history A to Z, "alpha" to "omega" is no man but the "Lord God . . . the Almighty". John's prophecy is characterised by a strongly evangelical view of God, and resembles strong statements of God found in other New Testament presentations of the gospel (for example, Acts 2:17–36; 17:24–31).

Second, in the doxology following the greeting, special reference is made to the third member of the triad, Jesus Christ, the one to whom God gave his revelation to make known to his servants through John. This is the person whom John chiefly brings before us. John gives us an astonishing wealth of information about Jesus Christ. That

Jesus is to be the focus of the reader's attention through-out the Revelation is made clear by the emphasis given to him in this the first part of the "book".

What is significant, in particular, is the evangelical character of these references. In the greeting, Jesus is *the faithful witness, the firstborn from the dead and the ruler of the kings of the earth* (v.5) Note the historical sequence as in other gospel-statements in the New Testament. He died as one who faithfully witnessed to the truth and the will of God. He was raised from death as the first of the many God will finally raise. He is now the ruler of the kings of the earth.

In the doxology Jesus' death is elaborated further. He *loves* us (note the present tense) and, in consequence, *has freed us from our sins* (the aorist verb tense signifies completed action). The thoroughly evangelical union of God's/Christ's love and Christ's saving death, so evident elsewhere in the New Testament (for example, Romans 5:8; 1 John 4:10), is also clearly seen here. The death of Jesus brings the closely related benefits of God's forgive-ness of sins and also his deliverance from their power in our lives. Through his blood (= his death) those who are believers have also been made ... a kingdom and priests to serve his God and father (note again the verb of com-pleted action). By means of Jesus' death we have become a "kingdom and priests" that is, a community ruled over by Jesus as King which continually offers to God the priestly sacrifices of prayer (cf 5:8). As elsewhere in the New Testament the death of Jesus is declared to be of incalculable value and power.

This powerfully evangelical greeting-doxology con-cludes, appropriately, with a strong statement affirming the return of Jesus. *Look, he is coming with the clouds and every eye will see him ... and all the peoples of the earth will mourn because of him* (v.7). John's reference to the climax of history, as the final element in the gospel, is paralleled in many other places within the New Testament (for example, Matthew 24:30).

Thus in the opening chapter of the Revelation the author designates his written "book" as the word of God ... the "testimony of/about Jesus" and as "prophecy". As we have noted, there are strong suggestions that he regarded his work as scripture and would have wished his readers to share that conviction. It is very significant, therefore, that we the readers are immediately reminded that the great blessings of grace and peace flow from a divine trinity and that we are overarched in history by the one who died, but who was raised back to life to be the ruler of his people and of kings and who will finally return at the end of history.

(2)   What John heard (1:9–11)

John now tells his readers about the first vision.

Although remote from the Asian Churches on lonely Patmos he identifies himself as their *brother*, their *companion* (literally fellow-sharer) in the *suffering*, the *kingdom* and the *patient endurance* that are his and theirs in Jesus. Specifically, John's confinement there was on account of the *word of God, the testimony of/about Jesus*. In other words the Roman proconsular authorities took exception to John's gospel-ministry in Asia and deported him to this remote island in the Aegean. Both he and the Asian churches, though physically separated, share in the common experience of suffering on account of their public witness to Jesus.

One *Lord's Day* (= Sunday) John was *in the Spirit*, that is either prophesying to other Christians on Patmos or engaged in some form of spiritual reflection or meditation. It was then that he was startled to hear the *trumpet-like* voice behind him directing him to write on a *scroll* the things he saw. This scroll was to be sent to the seven churches in the Asian cities. As suggested earlier, a messenger or *angel* (v.1) may have come from the Asian churches with messages and reports to John. It is possible that John heard the loud voice of Jesus soon after the visit of the messenger from the mainland. The revelation or prophecy which John came to write had its origin in the occasion when the trumpet-like voice addressed him.

(3) What John saw (1:12–20)

What did John see when he turned towards "the voice" ?

It was an amazing sight. Before him stood the *seven golden lampstands*, later identified as the seven churches of Asia which figure so prominently in the Revelation (1:20). *Among* (= in the midst of) the lampstands was, a human figure, *someone "like a son of man"*. These words derive from the Book of Daniel chapter 7. Daniel describes the evil, beast-like empires of the world as they rise and fall in succession. But then, finally, one "like a son of man" comes to the "Ancient of Days" (= God) who gives to that man-like person an everlasting dominion that will never pass away, a sovereignty over all peoples for all time. Here, then, in place of the transient empires of the world is a transcendent, permanent ruler, one who would be worshipped by all. It is this great figure whom John sees standing among the troubled churches. That the one "like a son of man" is described in terms appropriate for the "ancient of days", God, is John's way of depicting Jesus as a divine figure (v.14 cf Daniel 7:9).

44

The really significant thing is that Jesus himself adopted this unusual title; "son of man" was his preferred way of referring to himself. Clearly, therefore, Jesus saw himself as the one who would rule the nations; he constantly referred to himself in those terms. How encouraging it was for John (and for us) that the revelation of Jesus to John in *his* weakness and need was as the powerful "son of man" in the midst of his churches, in *their* weakness and need.

When John saw this person before him he *fell at his feet as though dead* (v.17). The total impact of his physical appearance and clothing was overpowering. The full-length *robe* as of a king, the *white hair* like that of the "Ancient of Days", Yahweh (Daniel 7:9) and the blazing, all-seeing *eyes* of the divine Judge drove John to kneel before this awesome figure. The fiery *bronze feet* of the conqueror, the thunderous, authoritative *voice*, the powerful *right hand* holding the *seven stars* (= the local church leaders?), the sword-like tongue in the *mouth* and the *face* brilliantly shining complete the image of the One who stood before John.

To John's immense relief this Judge-King reassuringly placed his *right hand* on him and spoke the following comforting words:

Do not be afraid.
I AM the First and the Last.
I AM the Living One.
I was dead, and behold
I AM alive for ever and ever.
I hold the keys of death and Hades. (vs. 17–18)

Jesus' deity is implied by the threefold I AM (see Exodus 3.14), by the title "Living One" and by his sovereignty over history as the "first and the last" in terms resembling "the Lord God . . . Almighty" (1:8).

45

Christ's *keys* to *death and Hades* (God's eternal punishment) are by virtue of his own victory over death. Though *dead* he is *alive for ever and ever.* Once again the completed, past victory of Christ is in mind. There is no future battle in prospect; the victory is already his. His absolute control over death and Hades is good news for John, for the churches and for us. He exercises that ultimate control over death, the last enemy (as Paul calls it) for our good.

Finally, the Risen One directs John to write what has been revealed to him:

what you have seen (= the circumstances of the seven churches: chapters 2–3),

what is (= the reality of God the Almighty and of the Lion/Lamb: chapters 4–5),

what is to come (= the things which are yet to occur in history: chapters 6–22).

These words form the natural divisions in the "book" John will now write:

Chapters 2–3 The seven churches ("what you have seen").

4–5 Worship in heaven of God and the Lamb ("what is").

6–22 The future ("what is to come").

John refers obliquely to *seven stars = the seven angels* of the churches (v.20). This mysterious reference may be to messengers from the churches who have perhaps come to Patmos to copy John's scroll and then to deliver and read it aloud to the constituent churches. These messengers are promised protection in the strong right hand of Jesus (cf 1:16).

QUESTIONS ON REVELATION CHAPTER I

1. John's readers were on the brink of trouble at the time he wrote (1:1,3). What might it have meant to take to heart the word of God at that time? What does the "messiah-like" presentation of many politicians reveal in our own age?

2. How does John's "prophetic" view of God (1:4,8) help readers faced with uncertainty and suffering? How best should we today encourage Christians who suffer physical persecution for their faith? How best might we prepare ourselves for times when we might be in similar circumstances?

3. How would what is said about Jesus in 1:5–7 have related
   a. to the original readers?
   b. and how does it encourage us?

4. What does it mean in practice to be a "kingdom and priests to serve his God" ?

5. What is the significance of the "son of man" standing among the "seven lampstands"?

6. What is meant by the description of Jesus' clothing, hair, eyes, and other parts of his body?

7. What might have been your reaction to Jesus' words to John in 1:7–18?

11

The Seven Churches in Asia 2–3

(1)   The pattern in the Seven Letters

As Leon Morris has shown (*Revelation,* p.58) there is a pattern which may be discerned in each of the seven letters.

1. The letter is directed to *the angel* (= the messenger who collected and will read the letter to the church).
2. *The words* which follow come from Jesus Christ, who is described in terms of the first Patmos vision, Revelation 1:12–16.
3. Jesus' *I know your* ... praises the good in each church (but not Laodicea).
4. His *but I have this against you* rebukes the churches for their shortcomings (but not Smyrna or Philadelphia).
5. A call to *repent* is accompanied by the exhortation *he who has an ear, let him hear.*
6. Jesus' encouragement *he who overcomes* is usually followed by an end-time promise from chapters 21–22.

(2)   The Seven Asian Churches

If you would like detailed background to the seven churches, refer to Colin Hemer, *The Letters to the Seven*

Churches of Asia in their Local Setting (University of Sheffield, 1986). Hemer believes that many of the references to these churches in these letters are made in terms of their local situations.

(i) Ephesus (2:1-7)

The city closest to Patmos, to which John's "book" would have been first been brought and read, was Ephesus, population 250,000. Its commercial greatness derived from its splendid location. A harbour port a short distance from the open sea, Ephesus was the natural depot not only for the hinterland to the north and south but, above all, to the great eastern trade routes which extended to Mesopotamia and the regions beyond. From this depot shipping could travel to the Black Sea, to other ports of the Aegean and, of course, to the greater world of the Mediterranean.

Regrettably for the city, the river in question, the Cayster, was subject to siltation and some centuries later the port of Ephesus was stranded about 10 kilometres inland, the river having finally disappeared. The extensive remains of ancient Ephesus, including the amphitheatre mentioned in the Acts of the Apostles, are sufficient to indicate how elegant a city it was in John's time.

Ephesus was at the time a *free city*, that is, having the right of self-government and not subject to direct Roman rule or military occupation. In terms of the law and judiciary it was an *assize city*. The Roman proconsul from the provincial capital, Pergamum, would make periodic visits there to deal with court cases which lay outside the jurisdiction of local magistrates. Through these proconsular visits Ephesus was reminded of the might of Rome by the pomp and pageantry associated with the governor's arrival.

The most notable feature of Ephesus, however, was its divine patron, the goddess Artemis (or Diana). The city's greatest pride was the massive temple devoted to Artemis which unfortunately has not survived the severe earthquakes which characterize the region. The religious practices based on the temple and the revenue generated by tourists and devotees dominated much of the city's day to day life.

The great temple, however, was also the source of the city's shame. From early times a right of asylum had been permitted to thieves, robbers and kidnappers, based on the sanctity of the shrine of Artemis, providing protection for all manner of criminals within the wider precincts of the city. More than one emperor in faraway Rome expressed concern at the evil effects of the protection granted malefactors by this asylum.

The church in Ephesus was more than 40 years old by this time. Jesus commends the members because they *have persevered and endured hardships* for Jesus' *name and have not grown weary* (2:3). They have tested and rejected as *false* the claims of certain *apostles*, whose identity is not known to us (2:2). Moreover, the Ephesian Christians *hate the practices of the Nicolaitans*, a movement within the churches (2:6,15) whose beliefs and practices are not clear to us today.

How would the authorities have viewed these Christians? As it happens two of the earliest references from non-Christians to the new faith come from about this time and from the very region to which the Revelation was directed. Neither writer is complimentary about Christianity. Tacitus, the great historian of imperial Rome who became Proconsul of Asia c.AD 110, said that Christians "hated the human race" and "were hated" by

the society in which they lived (*Annals* XV44). His friend
Pliny was governor of the adjoining province of Bithynia
at that time. In a famous letter to the Emperor Trajan,
Pliny describes Christianity as an "insanity", a "con-
tagion . . . a superstition" characterized by "obstinacy
and unbending perversity" (*Epistle* X). It is not too difficult to imagine how the Christians' steadfast refusal to
worship Rome and her emperor would have been seen so
negatively by these provincial governors.

Jesus rebukes the Ephesian Christians for having for-
saken their *first love* and calls on them to *remember the
height* from which they had *fallen* (2:4–5). Had their
initial enthusiasm for Jesus been replaced by a grim and
defensive orthodoxy?

To the one who *overcomes* ("conquers", RSV) in these
circumstances in Ephesus, Jesus makes promises that may
have had a particular impact in that city. Ephesus had
from earliest times revered a sacred tree which stood in
close proximity to the shrine of Artemis. Due to the
asylum offered criminals this tree was, in effect, a centre
for a rabble of evildoers. The faithful and penitent
Ephesian Christian is promised food from the *tree of life*,
a probable reference to the cross since the unusual word
"tree", *xylos*, is used elsewhere of the "accursed . . .
tree" on which Jesus died for sinners (Galatians 3:13; 1
Peter 2:24; Acts 5:30;10:39; 13:29).

Moreover, in the New Jerusalem – the *paradise of God*
– those who practise magic, the sexually immoral, the
murderers, the idolators and those who love and practise
falsehood will be *outside* not inside the walls (22:14–15).
Inside the city will be the faithful and holy ones who are
fed by the life-giving tree, the saving death of Jesus on
the cross. Jesus' promises are specially pertinent in light
of the sacred tree and the protection it rendered to evildoers in the city of Ephesus.

51

(ii) Smyrna (2:8–11)

Sixty kilometres to the north of Ephesus lay Smyrna, population 250,000. Located on a magnificent, easily defended harbour, Smyrna stood at the end of the Hermus valley. Like Ephesus it had very considerable maritime and overland trade passing through it. Also like Ephesus it was both a *free city* and an *assize city*. Smyrna was famous throughout the province and beyond for its town planning and architecture; it was known as "the glory of Asia". It boasted a famous stadium, a famous library, and the largest amphitheatre in Asia. There were impressive temples of Apollo, Asklepius, Aphrodite and for the Cybele mystery cult. It competed with and defeated Sardis for the honour of erecting a temple in honour of the Roman Emperor.

Jesus knows of the *poverty* (v.9) of the Smyrnaean Christians, something that was in stark contrast with the visible affluence of the city. In end-time terms, however, they were rich (v.9).

He speaks of the *slander* of those who say they are *Jews* (v.9). The Jewish people had suffered a crushing defeat from the Romans in Palestine 30 years earlier, the climax of which was the destruction of the Temple in Jerusalem AD 70. An added humiliation was that the tax previously paid by Jews for the upkeep of their Temple was now to be contributed for the temple of Jupiter in Rome. The large Jewish community in Smyrna, like others in the Roman world of the time, was deeply embittered in these circumstances. However, the Jews retained their protected status within the empire, the price for which was the temple tax. They were not compelled to participate in the numerous (pagan) religious ceremonies which were inherent in every aspect of domestic and municipal life. It appears from the Revelation that, in their bitterness, they took action against Christians both in Smyrna and Philadelphia (2:9; 3:9).

Christians were extremely vulnerable at that time since they could not, in conscience as Christians, participate in municipal pagan religion nor in worship of the emperor. From their protected position, however, Jews were able to "slander" the Christians as disloyal to the authorities and to Rome. John writes that they are not, in truth, Jews, not truly the people of God. Theirs is a *synagogue of Satan.* In their rejection of God's messiah, Jesus, and in their collaboration with pagan authorities against Christians they are really in league with Satan, not God.

In consequence of Jewish slander, Christians in Smyrna are about to *suffer. Prison, persecution* and *death* are mentioned by Jesus (vs.10–12). Presumably John has received up to date information on Patmos about the sufferings which are about to occur in Smyrna.

One who witnessed these events in Smyrna was Polycarp, a man then in his mid 20s, who had been taught the faith by the Apostle John. Within a few years he would become bishop of the church at Smyrna. Sixty years later, when he refused to renounce Jesus his king, he was condemned to the flames by the provincial governor. It is probably significant that the local Jewish community were actively involved in the burning of this Christian leader. Their bitterness against Christ and Christians was longlasting.

There are a number of references in the letter to Smyrna which seem particularly relevant for that city. That the church is addressed by One *who ... died and came to life again* (v.8) may have had a special point in a city which in preceding centuries had lost then regained its status as a city. One of Smyrna's emblems was the crown, making very appropriate the promise to the one who overcomes *I will give you the crown of life* (v.10).

Although Christians may suffer to the "point of death" in a gladiatorial arena, they will *not be hurt at all by the second death* (v.11 = hell. See 20:14).

(iii) Pergamum (2:12–17)

The road from Smyrna to the north proceeds parallel to the coast for 80 kilometres then turns inland 30 kilometres from the coast before coming to Pergamum. Its less advantageous geographic position did not allow it to assume the proportions or wealth of either Ephesus or Smyrna. Yet it was more famous than either of these cities. Pliny called Pergamum "by far the most famous city of Asia". In the aftermath of the subdivision of Alexander's empire, Pergamum became the capital of the Attalid Kingdom which ruled over the whole region that would later become the Roman province of Asia. In 133 BC its dying ruler bequeathed his realm to the Romans, who in turn recognised Pergamum as capital of Proconsular Asia. Although some argue that Ephesus became the capital, it is probable that Pergamum remained the capital of Asia.

The seat of the Roman governor was also, very significantly, the most important religious and cultic centre of the province. The ancient protectors of the city were Zeus and Athena. The deities Dionysus and Asklepius were also prominent. The Attalid kings had built great temples which were to be focal points for worship within the whole region. These kings fostered the cult of ruler-worship, focused on themselves in these many impressive temples.

In 29 BC Augustus permitted a temple for Rome and for himself to be erected in Pergamum. The worship of the Roman emperor as a living deity, which rapidly spread throughout the whole province, probably arose in

Pergamum. The emperor-cult quickly gained acceptance and was happily amalgamated with existing local cultic activities. It was in Pergamum that the high-priest of Asia was elected from the delegates of the other Asian cities. Fifteen years later in the nearby province of Bithynia the Governor Pliny describes the procedure for testing the loyalty of citizens to Rome. According to Pliny "they recited a prayer to the gods at my dictation, made supplication with incense and wine to [the emperor's] statue, which I had ordered to be brought in to the court for the purpose together with the images of the gods, and moreover cursed Christ . . . ". Pergamum was the cult centre of the province.

It is no surprise, therefore, that Jesus writes to those who lived in Pergamum *I know where you live — where Satan has his throne* (v.13). This is the second of many references to Satan within the Revelation. As the great red dragon Satan is cast down to the earth by the man child caught up to God (12:5,9) and he launches his assaults on believers in the form of two evil beasts (13:1,11). Such is the concentration of emperor-worship in Pergamum that Jesus says that it is *where Satan lives* (v.13). One person, Antipas by name, Jesus' *faithful witness*, was *put to death* in this city [in the recent past?]. Despite these grave problems, the Christians of Pergamum did *remain true* to Jesus' name; they did not deny Jesus during the crisis at the time of Antipas' death.

As if these were not difficulties enough there were no less than two forms of false teaching which had gained a foothold within the congregation at Pergamum. On one hand were those who held the teachings of Balaam (v.14), advocating compromise with the prevailing idolatry and sexual immorality of that society. The stern faithfulness of Antipas is in stark contrast with the capitulation to pagan standards of the so-called Balaam supporters. On the other hand in Pergamum we meet again the mysterious Nicolaitan teaching (v.15), which the Ephesian church had rejected, and which the Pergamenes had not.

Jesus promises to the one *who overcomes* in Pergamum, the city where Satan rules, the *hidden manna* and *a white stone with a new name written on it* (v17). Neither of these is simply understood and there has been much debate among the scholars about what is intended by these symbolic references. *Hidden manna* may refer to that "bread" of the end-time, by which God will feed his children in the New Jerusalem. As such it is in contrast with the Satanic "food" which the devotees of the emperor cult were required to eat in token of their loyalty to the Roman State. The *white stone* may have been a "ticket" giving admission to the gladiatorial games where, perhaps, Antipas gave his life for Jesus. The faithful will each have such a "stone", but with his or her own name on it, guaranteeing them access to the presence of God.

(iv) Thyatira (2:18–29)

The route implicit in the list of the seven churches now doubles back from Pergamum and strikes out inland, in a south easterly direction.

Thyatira is on the main road that went from Pergamum to Syria. It is the least important of the seven cities and one about which there is only limited information. It has not been subjected to archaeological investigation since it lies under an existing settlement.

Located at the meeting of well-travelled roads in a fertile valley it is assumed that Thyatira was a prosperous town. Lydia the trader in purple-dyed goods, a convert to Christianity 40 years earlier through Paul's ministry in Philippi, came from this town (Acts 16:14).

One of the most notable known facts about Thyatira was its relatively large number of trade-guilds and crafts and sports associations. Like the modern trade union, membership was *de facto* compulsory. The meetings of such groups inevitably involved cultic activities directed to both Anatolian as well as both Greek and Roman deities. While this letter makes no reference to pressure from the Emperor-Cult it is probable that membership in the merchants' and other associations would have involved considerable conflict for Christians.

Apart from a shrine to the goddess Samathe little is known of Thyatira's religious and cultic activity.

Jesus warmly acknowledges the Thyatirans' *love, faith-*[fulness], *service* and *perseverance* and that they are *doing more* now *than . . . at first* (v.19).

Nonetheless, there is a major problem in the church in Thyatira. The so-called "teaching of Balaam", which also had adherents within the adjoining church at Pergamum, is tolerated by the Thyatirans as a whole, and actively practised by a number of the members. This "teaching", which promotes the eating of food offered to idols and sexual immorality, possibly arose directly out of the immoral cultic worship in the local temples or perhaps from the trade-guilds.

The leading advocate of this teaching in Thyatira is actually a prophetess from within the church. She is referred to as *"Jezebel"* (v.20) after Ahab's evil queen who attempted to introduce the worship of pagan deities to Israel (1 Kings 16:31). It is not clear whether the reference to those who *commit adultery with her* and *her children* (vs.22,23) is literal or metaphorical. In all probability it is a metaphorical reference and probably ties in with *Satan's deep secrets* (v.24), which sound like secret initiatory rites of an immoral religious cult. Either way dire punishment awaits those mentioned unless they *repent*. That **all the churches will know** that Jesus is the One who *searches the hearts and minds* and that he *will repay each according to his deeds* (v.23) probably indicates that Thyatira may have been the evil well-spring of the "teaching of Balaam" from which it had flowed to other churches like Pergamum.

The one who *overcomes* in Thyatira and does Jesus' *will to the end* is promised, in the language of Psalm 2, to share with the Son of God in his kingly *rule* and *authority* over *the nations* (vs.26–27). This is the unimaginable rule exercised by those who remain true to Jesus over those who oppress them. It is the triumph of goodness, hope and courage in the face of malice and evil and it was exemplified in the manner of Jesus' own death. How is the Son of God's rule and authority mediated to the nations? The answer of the Revelation would be: through the "word of God and the testimony of/about Jesus". Jesus rules the nations by the gospel courageously presented.

There is the further promise of the *morning star* (v.28), a puzzling reference. The most probable explanation relates to the Old Testament character Balaam, whose teaching (metaphorically speaking) is so entrenched in Thyatira. Despite being a sorcerer and false-prophet, the original Balaam did speak of "a star" that would arise from among God's people and rule the nations (Numbers 24:17). For centuries the Jews had looked for the coming of this "star". So famous was the prophecy that the Greeks and Romans were also very interested in the identity of this ruler from the east. Jesus the speaker is that "morning star" and he will be the gift to those who remain faithful to him.

(v) Sardis (3.1–6)

The road from Pergamum proceeds through Thyatira about 50 kilometres to Sardis. This important city was at the junction of five roads: to the north west to Pergamum, to the west 80 kilometres to Smyrna, to the south west 100 kilometres to Ephesus, to the south east 50 kilometres to Philadelphia and due east into the centre of Phrygia and beyond. The city's wealth and historical importance was due to its central location and to the general fertility of the region. The city was built on the high point of a mountainous ridge, giving it control over the whole surrounding region. In the distant past major battles had been fought in and near Sardis. Sardis was the eastern extremity of Hellenized civilization; beyond lay the wilds of Lydia.

In the more recent past, in AD 17, Sardis had been severely damaged by a major earthquake. The city regained its former grandeur as a result of the generous benefaction of the Emperor Tiberius.

It is significant that no hint is given in this letter of either external oppression or of internal compromise through false teaching. We would perhaps expect that, in these circumstances, the Sardian Christians would have attracted the commendation of Jesus. But this is not the case. In point of fact no church is so sharply rebuked as the church in Sardis. Despite their *reputation for being alive*, the reality was that they were *dead* (v.1). The members are called on to *wake up*, to *strengthen what remains, to repent* (vs.2–3). The greater majority have *soiled clothes* (v.4), a reference to their moral and spiritual compromise. Only a few are faithful, *dressed in white* (v.5). He who *overcomes*, Jesus *will acknowledge before his Father and his angels* (v.5), a clear reference to words spoken by the historic Jesus and recorded in the Gospels (for example, Mark 8:38).

(vi) Philadelphia (3:7–13)

Continuing down the great south east road which left Pergamum and passed through Thyatira we come to Philadelphia, about 50 kilometres beyond Sardis. Philadelphia, a relatively new city, arose during the Hellenistic era. The road from Sardis forked at Philadelphia, one route proceeding on in a south easterly direction to Laodicea, the other going due east into the region of Phrygia. Like Sardis, but perhaps to a greater degree, Philadelphia was a frontier city, a last bastion of Greek civilization. Some scholars believe that Philadelphia had a "missionary" role and that it existed to send the message of Greek civilization to the wild tribespeople of the interior of Asia Minor. This may help explain why the risen Christ tells the Philadelphian Church *Behold, I have set before you an open door* (v.8). Did the Church have an analogous missionary role: an open door through which to bring the message of Christ to these remote peoples? But the "opened door" may also refer to the believers' access into heaven spoken of at the beginning of the fourth chapter.

As in Smyrna the Jews are a source of grave difficulty for the Christians of Philadelphia. Reference to them and *the Synagogue of Satan* (v.9) is followed immediately by the ominous warning about the *hour of trial that is about to come upon the whole world to test those who live on earth* (v.10). Punishment by the Roman authorities for failure to participate in the emperor-cult appears to have arisen as a direct result of Jewish complaints and reports to the local officials.

Possibly Christians had sought to hide from the demands of the emperor-cult by belonging to the synagogue. (It will be remembered that the Jews' payment of the temple tax for the Temple of Jupiter in Rome after AD 70 was in effect the price of freedom to continue worshipping the God of Israel.) Why would the Jews one day *fall down* at [Christians'] *feet and acknowledge that* [Jesus had] *loved them*? Was it because Christians had pleaded in vain to the Jews of the synagogue in Philadelphia not to turn them in to the authorities as Christians?

The city of Philadelphia was economically weak, due to two major problems. One was the continuing seismic activity that affected the region to which Philadelphia belonged. Like Sardis, Philadelphia had been destroyed in the great earthquake of AD 17. The people were often forced to leave the city and then engage in extensive rebuilding on their return. The other difficulty was the Emperor Domitian's curb of vine growing as decreed in AD 92, which was designed to promote greater cultivation of corn within the empire. This city was gravely affected by this policy since it was the largest grape growing region in the province. Many people were uprooted from the region as a result of this imperial decree.

Jesus' promises to the one who overcomes, to the one who endures patiently, are couched in terms that may have had particular relevance to the local people. First, by analogy with the time-honoured practice of dedicating a commemorative pillar in a temple in honour of a local citizen, Jesus will make the one who overcomes *a pillar in the temple of God in the new Jerusalem which is coming down out of heaven.* The promise *never again will he leave* that temple is probably a pointed reference to the frequent departure from Philadelphia to escape the perils

61

of earthquakes on the one hand, and the forced emigration of those affected by the grape growing ban, on the other. Life in Philadelphia was very uncertain, but there would be security in the City of God.

The other promise, *I will write on him my new name* (v.12), probably points to the renaming of the city Neocaesarea in honour of Tiberius whose generosity to the earthquake-affected cities of the area in AD 17 had made possible their rebuilding.

The notorious schism known as Montanism arose in Phrygia, at whose frontier Philadelphia stood. This movement was based, in part, on literal interpretation of the Revelation, including that the New Jerusalem would actually descend on nearby Pepuza, the home of the founder, Montanus. Literal interpretation of Revelation had the effect then, as it has always done, of bringing the book into disrepute and neglect with the wider community of Christians.

(vii) Laodicea (3:14–22)

Laodicea, the last of the seven Asian cities, is located about 160 kilometres east of Ephesus, the first-mentioned city. The journey from Laodicea to Ephesus completes the circuit implied in the list of churches.

This city is situated near the point where the Maeander river is joined by its tributary, the Lycus. Whereas the narrow Lycus valley running to the south east is the gateway to the region of Phrygia, the great Maeander flows westwards through its broad valley finally entering the Aegean close to Miletus, the mainland city closest to the island of Patmos. The city lay at the junction of the great north-south road linking Pergamum to Attalia with the main trade route from Ephesus to the East. Laodicea's location relative to rivers and roads made her one of the major cities of Asia and a great commercial centre by world standards.

Laodicea lay between two other cities within the Lycus valley, Hierapolis 10 kilometres to the north and plainly visible from Laodicea, and Colossae 17 kilometres to the southeast. Christianity came to the three towns in the region more than 40 years earlier through Epaphras, a native of Colossae, who was an associate of Paul's during the apostle's ministry in Ephesus in the middle 50s (see Acts 19:1, 8–10; Colossians 1:7; 2:1; 4:12–13). Christ identifies himself as the *ruler of God's creation*, a phrase similar to one used in Paul's letter to nearby Colossae (cf also "firstborn from the dead" in Revelation 1:5; Colossians 1:18). Pauline teaching to the Lycus churches appears to have been known to John, despite his isolation on Patmos.

Papias, the bishop of Hierapolis during the first quarter of the next century, and an early witness to Peter's involvement in the writing of the Gospel of Mark, was probably a member of the churches of the Lycus at that time. He, like his friend and contemporary, Polycarp of Smyrna, appears to have been instructed in the Christian faith by the apostle John. Papias and Polycarp became the leaders of the Asian Churches in the first generation after the great apostle, that is, in the first decades of the second century.

Like its counterpart in Sardis, the Church of Laodicea does not appear to have been troubled either by the external pressure of the emperor-cult nor by the distractions caused internally by false teachers. The problem in Laodicea was that the quality of church life did not match the church's own high opinion of itself. The church at Laodicea was mediocre, as lukewarm and vomit-inducing as water from the hot springs in nearby Hierapolis. It was, moreover, mineral laden and very unpleasant to taste.

As with other towns in that seismically-active region, Laodicea had suffered severe damage from earthquakes. Unlike Philadelphia and Sardis, however, which had received generous imperial assistance to rebuild after major earthquakes, Laodicea had declined outside help. In AD 60 Laodicea suffered extensive damage but the citizens themselves reconstructed their city. Something of this indigenous Laodicean pride in achievement appears to have blinded the perceptions of the church about their own lukewarmness. According to the Risen One the church in Laodicea said *"I am rich; I have acquired wealth and do not need a thing"*. His verdict, however, was *But you do not realize that you are wretched, pitiful, poor, blind and naked*. The church in Laodicea is called on to receive from Christ, not from within themselves, *gold . . . white clothes and eye-salve*. These words come with particular force when it is realized that Laodicea was a significant banking centre, and a noted producer of both woollen cloth and remedial ointment for eye ailments.

It is to this church, perhaps the least attractive of the seven, that Jesus makes his gracious promise to the members. *I stand at the door and knock*, he says, *. . . if anyone opens . . . I will go in and eat with him*. Jesus will give to this church, and indeed to all others that ask, what it cannot give to itself, namely the qualities of faithfulness and love, which will make it worthy of his name.

(3) Jesus and his promise to the churches

Against the pretentious claims of Domitian Caesar and his local provincial representatives the Risen Christ addresses his churches in Asia in the following terms. He is the First and the Last who died and came to life, the Son of God with flaming eyes and feet of burnished bronze, the I AM who searches mind and heart, the Holy One, the True One with the key of David, the Faithful and True Witness, and the Beginning of God's Creation. He has fought and won his great battle in crucifixion and resurrection; now he is seated in triumph with his Father on his throne. How petty and small the merely human emperor is next to this majestic figure.

He calls his churches to repent of lovelessness, of mediocrity, of false teaching and of godless behaviour. Repeatedly he exhorts their members to resist the extreme local pressure to bow the knee to the emperor and the gods in the worship of the pagan temples in the cities. The writings of Tacitus and Pliny, to which we have referred, show us something of the hostility which the local people and their officials felt towards these believers. On each occasion he encourages them to conquer, to win through, as he has, against powerful opposition. To those who do triumph against these forces he promises the fruit of the tree of life, deliverance from the second death (= hell), and a sharing in his rule over the nations. These great promises are expanded upon in the vision of the New Jerusalem in chapters 21–22.

QUESTIONS ON REVELATION
CHAPTERS 2–3.

1. What are the things which Jesus commends in the
   seven churches?
   2:2–3
   2:9
   2:13
   2:19
   3:8

2. What are the things which Jesus criticises in the
   churches?
   2:4
   2:14–15
   2:20
   3:1
   3:15,17

3. In what ways do the social and political characteristics of these regions or cities bear resemblance to our
   own?

4. What warnings and encouragements are there in
   these passages for your church?

5. What are Jesus' encouragements here to faithfulness
   in your own life?

12

Heaven opened 4–5

The grim circumstances of the seven churches of
Proconsular Asia are now behind us. Once again John
hears the trumpet-like voice, not behind him as
previously, but from above. Before John is *a door
standing open*, the Greek perfect tense signifying that,
once opened, the door is now always open. Through
Christ's atoning death we now have permanent access
to heaven and to God. The pain of earth experienced
in the seven churches as set out in chapters two and
three is followed by the peace of heaven described in
chapters four and five.

John is invited into the presence of God so that the
Speaker may show him *what must take place after this*
(v.1 cf 1:19). The destiny of humanity and of God's
people is about to be unrolled before John's eyes: fearful
images of tyranny, chaos, persecution and destruction.
However, before John is taken on this awesome earthly
journey, which will occupy chapters six to twenty, he is
given a majestic vision of heaven.

(1) A throne in heaven (4:2–6)
John does not explain the meaning of *in the Spirit* (v.2 cf

1.10; 21:10). As a prophet (22:9) we may say he was conscious that what he saw in his mind was given to him by the Spirit of God; it was not his own imagination.

Before him was a *throne*, a seat from which a king rules. With due reverence and in obedience to the Second Commandment no description of the Enthroned One is given, merely the colourful impression of a majestic presence. *He who sat there **appeared** like* (v.3 RSV) the green coloured precious stone *jasper* and the red coloured stone *carnelian*. No human features are ascribed to the Almighty One.

Nearest the throne and encircled (or overarched by it) was the *emerald*-like *rainbow*, reminding us of the sign of mercy given by God after the primeval deluge in promise that he would not again destroy the earth by water (Genesis 9:15,16). The rainbow teaches us that God is majestic in the qualities of faithfulness and covenant mercy by which he rules his people. His promises to them will never fail.

In a circle, facing the throne were *twenty four thrones* on which were seated *twenty four elders* (v.4). These symbolize the people of God from the Old and New Testaments: twelve tribes of Israel and twelve disciples/apostles. That they sit on *thrones*, are dressed in *white* and wear *crowns* show us that they have been victorious in loyalty to their God despite enormous opposition during their lifetimes. Raised from the dead in the first resurrection (= when Christ rose from the dead) the people are in the very presence of their God, whose rule they now share. What is the nature of their co-rule with God? It is that they have been given authority to share with God in judging individuals and nations in the final, great judgment of God (see 20:4).

The *flashes of lightning* and the *peals of thunder* that issue from the throne (v.5) speak of that coming judgment. While it is good to be reminded of the rainbow and the covenant mercy of God it is important not to forget that the majestic Enthroned One is also the Judge of all people.

In front of the throne were *blazing* (present tense) *seven lamps*, the seven *Spirits of God*, the number seven signifying divine perfection. This is the powerful, omnipresent Spirit whom God sends into the farthest recesses of time and space to do his will and to convict the consciences of men and women and to draw them into his kingdom.

Before the throne was what *looked like a sea of glass, clear as crystal* (John does not actually say what it was, only what it looked like). Elsewhere in the Revelation the sea (Greek: *thalassa*) is the abode of evil (see 13:1) and the lake (Greek: *limen*) is the place of punishment of the enemies of God (see 19:20; 20:10,14,15). But the sea also reminds us of the Red Sea through which God delivered his people. Later John will describe faithful believers as having emerged triumphant from "what looked like a sea of glass mixed with fire" (15:2) singing the Song of Moses (15:3). The twenty four elders, symbolizing the triumphant people of God, have now emerged from the fiery sea of affliction and persecution into the presence of their God. This beautiful, peaceful, sea-like expanse before the throne is meant to portray the stillness and majesty of the final victory of God. The fire in the sea is no more; all conflict is now passed. There are few things so quietly beautiful as the glass-like sea untroubled by wind, as seen in the first light after the dawn. Let its beauty speak to us of what John saw beyond the opened door.

(2)   The four living creatures (4:6-8)

These four animals symbolize the noblest (*lion*), the strongest (*ox*), the wisest (*human*) and the swiftest (*eagle*) living beings created by God. Their many *eyes* speak of the insight into their source of existence and survival. These eminent spokemen of the created order know what humanity for all its knowledge does not know: that the Lord God Almighty is the One who was and is and is to come; he, and no mere human is the Eternal One, overarching history.

Like the seraphim of Isaiah 6.2 who each have *six wings* these beings also affirm that God is *holy, holy, holy.* On earth human power is associated with evil, at least to some degree. Power is achieved by evil means and exercised for evil ends. Roman rule from top to bottom, as wielded by the emperor or his lowliest bureaucrat, was tinged with corruption and self-interest. John's readers in the churches in Roman Asia knew in the pain of their own experience that power and authority were the incarnation of evil. The Emperor Domitian demanded to be worshipped as "Lord and God". As the citizens of Asia gathered in the various temples for cultic meals and ceremonies they solemnly declared before the statues of gods and mortals the deity of the Princeps and of the Roman State. But these mere creatures who stand before the Enthroned One, full of eyes (= insight), never stop declaring the holiness, that is the uncompromised purity and goodness of the Lord God Almighty. He, not the emperor, is the ruler of history, the One who was and is and is to come (v.8).

(3)   The twenty four elders (4:9-11)

The Revelation has many songs or hymns which are characterised by a two-beat rhythm. The first beat in this

instance is the evangelical proclamation of the four creatures that *holy, holy, holy* is the Lord God Almighty. (If
you doubt that this is part of the evangel = gospel, see
chapter 14:6–7).

The second beat is the worshipful response of the
twenty four elders representing the redeemed people of
God. Whenever they hear the declaration of the four
creatures they *fall down* and *worship*, not the Roman
Emperor, but *him who sits on the throne, who lives for
ever and ever.* These *lay their crowns* before his throne in
acknowledgement that God alone is King. It is not
Domitian but *our Lord and God ... who is worthy to
receive glory, honour and power.*

Worship is not to be thought of, primarily, in either
aesthetic or emotional terms, though aesthetics and the
emotions may be involved. Worship is the expression of
agreement by the people of God about the truth of God.
Worship is based on the evangelical declaration about
who God is, and what God does.

This two beat pattern may be seen in the words of the
twenty four elders. They begin by declaring God to be
worthy to receive glory, honour and power. Then, in
reverse order, they state the evangelical truth which is
the basis for their worship of God. It is because (Greek:
hoti = for) by his will God *created all things* that they
declare God to be *worthy of glory, honour and power.*

(4)   The scroll of destiny (5:1–4)

We come now to a critical point. The scroll held in the
right hand of the Enthroned One would tell the story of
the world's future. It is full of information being written
on both sides of the scroll, on the inside and the outside.
Seven seals prevent its message being read.

But only a special person may open this scroll. Who-
ever knows its secrets knows the hidden mind of God.

71

Moreover, the one who opens the seals becomes the agent by which the hitherto hidden plans of God are executed. Hence a mighty angel issues a challenge in a *loud voice* that penetrates to the whole creation: *who is worthy to break the seals and open the scroll*? There is silence; no reply is heard. No one is worthy. John himself weeps profusely since without a worthy person, the future, including the blessings of the New Heaven and New Earth will not be known, will not come to pass. The dragon and his evil beasts will continue to maul and attack the people of God.

(5) *The Lion of the tribe of Judah (5.5–7)*

One of the twenty four *elders*, representing the re-deemed people of God, told John *do not weep*. There *is* someone worthy to open the scroll. The elder pointed to one who was present: *the lion of the tribe of Judah, the root of David*. This is a description of the long-awaited Messiah, the Lord's anointed, who would descend from King David and, therefore, belong to the tribe of Judah. But only here in the whole of scripture is the Anointed One called "the Lion".

Three things should be noted about the verb *triumphed* (= "conquered" RSV; Greek: *enikesen*):

(i) It comes as the first word in the sentence, for empha-sis.

(ii) There is no object, reflecting the absolute nature of the victory.

(iii) The aorist tense indicating a completed action shows that the great battle of God is not in the future but in the past and that it has been fought and won.

Here was hope for John and his pathetic readers in Asia, on whom all the evil wrath of Roman imperial might was soon fully to descend. Here to open the scroll was a conqueror, a Lion.

When at last John looked in the direction the elder pointed, however, he did not see a lion. Rather, he saw an animal unimaginably different from a lion; he saw a lamb. Before him stood not a powerful, noble beast, who would conquer for them but, of all things, a young sheep, and what is even worse one so severely wounded that it would soon die. The lamb was *as if it had been slain.* Yet this mortally wounded Lamb was in a place of great prominence, *I saw a Lamb ... standing in the centre of the throne*, encircled by the *four living creatures and the elders*. Soon these will fall down in worship before the Lamb.

Here we note a characteristic of the author's style. The Lamb with the death wound clearly represents Jesus the crucified Son of God. Yet the passage goes on immediately to speak of his sovereign power. The Lamb has *seven horns*, signifying divine power, and *seven eyes*, pointing to divine knowledge (v.6). The Lamb is at once both crucified and powerful. John appears to have in his mind fixed, evangelical realities about Jesus (namely his death and resurrection) which he portrays symbolically as the Lamb's death-wound on the one hand, and by its seven horns and seven eyes, on the other.

(6)   Worthy is the Lamb (5:7–14)

A moment of high drama follows. The Lion who triumphed was said to be worthy to take the scroll. Yet the Lion is not seen nor ever heard of again in Revelation; only the Lamb with the death-wound. The Messianic Son of David is the divinely appointed conqueror, but only in respect of his death. It is not the Lion as Lion who takes the scroll of destiny; it is the Lion as the Lamb looking as if it had been slain, who takes scroll. J.P. Love points out that: "None but an inspired composer of heavenly visions would ever have thought of it. When earth-bound men want symbols of power they conjure up mighty beasts and birds of prey. Russia elevates the bear, Britain the lion, France the tiger, the United States the eagle — all of them ravenous. It is only the kingdom of heaven that would dare to use as its symbol of might not the lion for which John was looking but the helpless lamb, and at that, a slain lamb" (*Commentary on 1,2,3 John, Jude, Revelation*, SCM Layman's Series).

The moment the Lamb took the scroll the four living creatures and the twenty four elders *fell down before the Lamb*. This, we note in passing, is evidence of his deity; only the Lord God was to be worshipped (Deuteronomy 6:13). In the hands of the elders are the *golden bowls full of incense, the prayers of the saints* (v.8), so apparently useless on earth, yet so precious in heaven.

Creatures and elders, representing both the orders of creation and redemption, unite in *a new song*, an evangelical declaration of praise to the Lamb. The only person in heaven or earth, the only person throughout the length and breadth of history fit to be entrusted with God's secret plans and to execute them within history is the Lamb. But why? What is it that qualifies the Lamb alone for this unique honour? The words of creatures and elders are instructive. *You are worthy to take the scroll and open its seals*, they sing, **because** you were slain . . . (v.9).

Is it then the martyr's death that qualifies the lamb to take the scroll and open its seals ? By no means. The song continues

*and with your blood you **purchased** men for God . . . you have made them to be a kingdom and priests to serve our God.*

The Lamb's death, though representing an everlasting example of faithfulness to God, achieved a real freedom and a new status for those who avail themselves of its benefits. The basis of the Lamb's authority, then, is that his death was paid as a ransom price to purchase men and women for God. Formerly they had been captives to sin and to the power the evil one exercised over them. The death of Jesus is the means by which these have changed ownership. They no longer belong to Satan; now they are the people of God, his Kingdom. The Lamb that was slain has constituted them as a realm or kingdom ruled now by God. Through their prayers they are priests who serve God. Although severely disadvantaged and entirely powerless within their society they actually reign on earth. They reign in the way Christ "reigned" during the crucifixion. It is a reign of courage, of love, of truth and of hope; qualities that come from God himself and which are greater than death. The person possessed of these qualities, though poor and powerless, has the dignity of Christ the king. There is no race on earth or within history unaffected by the killing of the Lamb. He redeemed individuals from every *tribe . . . nation . . . people . . .* and *language.*

Once more we have the two–beat rhythm, the response of confession and worship to the evangelical declaration. Encircling the throne, the living creatures and the elders are innumerable angels who sing in a loud voice *Worthy is the Lamb that was slain to receive power . . . wealth . . . wisdom . . . strength . . . honour . . . glory . . . praise.* Then, drowning even that great sound John heard every creature, animal and human, from earth and sea, singing *to him who sits on the throne* and also *to the Lamb . . . praise . . . honour . . . glory . . . and power for ever and ever.*

This could easily be regarded as the climax of the whole book of Revelation. Can we imagine this scene?

Here is the whole of creation, gathered together and joining together in an indescribable hymn of praise to the Enthroned One and to the Lamb. It will be remembered that mass rallies, with dazzling ceremonial, stirring singing and incredible oratory took pre-war Germany by storm. It was the worship of naked power and blind nationalism. In Roman society of that time, including within the province of Asia, there were tumultuous public occasions in which emperors were acclaimed and worshipped. But why does all creation gather in worship of God and the Lamb? It is for good things, not bad. It is to acknowledge from the heart that God is good, loving and true and that, through his Son, he redeems people from the powers of evil and destruction. As the whole creation converges on the throne to revere and praise God, so we, the people of God gather week by week to express the double-beat rhythm of evangelical proclamation and hearty worship of the triune God who has redeemed us.

QUESTIONS ON REVELATION CHAPTERS 4–5:

1. What do we learn of God firstly by the choice of these colourful images (4:3), and secondly by the fact that no more specific details were provided?

2. What do the four creatures know that humanity does not (4:7–8)?

3. Why is worship offered to God *and* to the Lamb?

4. The Lion who conquered is the Lamb that was slain. What does this teach us about (a) the character of Jesus, and (b) our own walk of obedience?

5. How does the nature and purpose of God's power differ from that of Satan?

13

Tyranny 6-7

The Lamb has now taken the sealed scroll from the right hand of the Enthroned One.

Human destiny is about to be revealed. Four sequences will pass before us dealing respectively with tyranny, chaos, persecution and destruction.

These sequences, however, are not to be understood as occurring consecutively within history. Rather they occur concurrently. It may be helpful to liken them to the plastic transparencies on which words are written or pictures drawn which are then displayed on a screen by an overhead projector. On one transparency is symbolically depicted tyranny within history, on another chaos, on another persecution, on another destruction. As we reflect on life we find ourselves surrounded by tyranny, chaos, persecution and destruction, though to varying degrees, depending which point it is within history we are examining. The images are all mixed together. The transparencies are piled on top of each other and, as the light of various hues is shone through them, our own social and historical context is formed before us in apocalyptic images. What John does — and we shall not understand his book if we don't grasp this — is to separate these four themes and examine them in turn. What we may not do is place the sequences in line and treat them as a preview or prophecy of specific events which we must then by our inspired ingenuity attempt to identify!

Another aspect of John's method which must also be understood is his division of each sequence into seven parts. The sequence on tyranny, for example, describes the removal of seven seals from a scroll. The seventh seal doesn't really belong to its sequence but serves as a bridge to bring us into the next, in this case the sequence of the seven trumpets. Each sequence concludes, in effect, with an interlude following the sixth part. The interludes in the sequences mostly focus on the blessings of heaven and the new age.

(1) Tyranny: four evil horsemen (6:1–8)

There is a tragic sequence here. Since the colour white as used by John signifies conquest, the *white horse* points to the military-minded ruler setting out to invade the homelands of others and make them his own. Appropriately the rider held a *bow* and wears a *crown*, symbolizing respectively warfare and kingly rule.

The second horse is *fiery red* signifying the fighting and the battles which inevitably follow once the white horse and its rider have set out. Its rider wields a *large sword* and he *takes peace from the earth.*

The black horse symbolizing famine and deprivation comes next. His rider holds *a set of scales* and a voice is heard saying that a mere handful of wheat costs a day's wages to purchase. Hunger and disease are implicit in the opening of this seal.

Following the other three come the evil pale horse (Greek: *chloros* = chlorine, or green/grey in colour). This is the colour of the human corpses who mark the inescapable finale of the awful sequence begun by the white horse. Its rider is named *Death* and *Hades* (= "hell" which follows death). A quarter of humanity is killed by *sword, famine, plague and wild beasts.*

Unlike many before and since, John is utterly frank and unromantic about war. He knows that whenever a ruler is bent on conquest, whenever the white horse and its rider come forth on the stage of history, these tragic consequences follow. His vivid realism will prove to be as true at the time of Genghis Khan as they were during the epoch of Adolph Hitler. The surviving black and white newsreel footage of the horrors of World War II, or the television coverage of the bloody Viet-Nam war, provide unforgettable cinematic images which confirm John's apocalyptic images of the four garishly coloured horses and their grim riders. Tyranny and war, however, are by no means confined to the news headlines. There are up to one hundred conflicts occurring in the world at this very time, during what is called a "post-war" period, each bringing its own measure of suffering.

John, however, is probably referring to tyranny in his own life time and experience, that is, to the conquest and warfare waged by the legions of Imperial Rome. Both John and his readers must have known of the devastating Roman invasion of Galilee and Judaea which began thirty years earlier in AD 66 at the command of the Emperor Nero. Many of John's readers, as Christian Jews, had probably fled from the war zone and made new lives in proconsular Asia. The historian Josephus, an eyewitness of these events, tells how dwellings and synagogues were destroyed, the Temple demolished, vineyards, fruit trees, and other vegetation uprooted and tens of thousands of men, women and children put to the sword. Josephus narrates how captive Jewish patriots were slaughtered by

wild animals in the amphitheatres of the Graeco-Roman
cities of Palestine. He also notes how the most prized of
the Jewish resistance leaders were shipped to Rome and
publicly butchered as the climax of the triumphal march
through the streets of Rome. John and his readers had
good reason to think of the aggression and savagery of
Imperial Rome in terms like those of the four horses and
their riders.

Despite John's grim realism about the naked power of
the regime under which he lived, a realism true of many
subsequent power-worshipping kingdoms down to our
own times, his words are full of comfort. According to
John, the horses emerge from the scroll not at their own
volition but because the Lamb breaks the seals on the
scroll and God's faithful living creatures issue the command "come".

As so often in the biblical text the passive voice is used
in reverence for the name of God. Thus the words "*a
crown . . . was given, a rider was given power to take
peace from the earth . . . was given a great sword, Death
and Hades were given power over a quarter of the earth*"
all indicate clearly that the sovereign *God* gave these
things. In the midst of the tragedy and pain caused by the
tyrant, God remains in control. His mercy may be seen in
the preservation of the everyday necessities *oil and wine*,
even though wheat is in desperately short supply and
shockingly overpriced. Divine mercy also restricts the
destruction to one quarter of humanity. It is a severe
mercy, yet mercy nonetheless, that spares three quarters
of the people from the depredations of the tyrant.

(2)   The cry of the martyrs (6:9–11)

Christians have often been among those killed under the
regime of the tyrant, as was the German scholar Dietrich

Bonhoeffer during the latter part of World War II. Immediately in John's mind, however, are those who have perished at the hands of the tyrant, Imperial Rome.

Up to the time of the great fire of Rome in AD 64 Roman authorities had treated Christians as circumscribed within Judaism. Gallio the Proconsul of Achaea, for example, told Paul's Jewish accusers in Corinth around AD 51, that they, not the Roman authorities, must "settle the matter" in question since it was an internal concern of the Jews (Acts 18:12–15). Since the Jews alone enjoyed the freedom not to worship the Roman gods it was to the Christians' great advantage that the Romans perceived them to be a denomination or sect within Judaism. This perception was to change. The first evidence of this was that Christians were attacked *as Christians* in the aftermath of the great fire in Rome. They were no longer able to shelter under the umbrella of Judaism.

On that occasion, according to Tacitus: "large numbers . . . dressed in wild animal skins . . . were torn to pieces by dogs, or crucified, or made into torches to be ignited after dark as substitutes for daylight . . ." (*Annals* xv, 44). From that time Christians were utterly vulnerable to attack by the authorities. Failure to worship the emperor and the gods at the demand of the provincial authorities would mean severe punishment or death. The tyrant who takes peace from the earth is also the persecutor of those who withhold their worship from him. It is clear that Christians in proconsular Asia were at the mercy of those Jews who chose to give the names of Christians to the authorities. The evidence from the Revelation suggests that Christians had been put under great pressure in recent times and that a great onslaught against them was imminent.

Those ... slain because of the word of God and the testimony they had maintained (v.9), therefore, probably refers to the ones who have lost their lives as Christians during and since the time of Nero. Clearly, they are exactly the same ones referred to later as those *"who had been beheaded because of their testimony for Jesus and because of the word of God"* (20:4). (The souls of the martyrs *under the altar* refers to their eternal protection by God. See 8:3.)

Although slain, these faithful ones are alive. They are to be identified with the beheaded ones mentioned above who we are later told *"came to life and reigned with Christ a thousand years ... who have a part in the first resurrection"* (20.4). God's gift to them of a white robe (v.11) signifies their victory, a victory also symbolized in the later passage by the thrones on which they are seated. Through their faithfulness to Jesus they are alive and rule with Christ throughout the entire period be-tween the "first resurrection" and the "second death", an epoch symbolically referred to as "a thousand years" (see 20:5,6,14). The question *how long ... until you ... avenge our blood?* is not a request for indiscriminate vengeance but for the justice of the *Sovereign Lord, holy and true* to be applied to those whose injustice and cru-elty has destroyed these innocent lives.

The Lord's sovereignty is implied in his answer that they must *wait ... until the number* of those *who were to be killed as they had been was completed.* The times and the numbers are in God's hands.

(3) The wrath of the Lamb (6:12–17)

The sixth seal, which the Lamb opens, heralds the great judgment of God on the tyrant-persecutors. We don't have to wait to the end of the Revelation to read about the final visitation of the wrath of God; it is described within this, the first of the sequences. *The great day of . . . wrath has come.* But this will be found in many later references as well.

Those who are depicted as seeking to escape their just deserts are the very ones represented in the first four seals, the war-mongering tyrant and his minions. John speaks of them as the *kings of the earth, the princes, the generals, the rich, the mighty, and every slave and every free man.* These are the client kings, military commanders, the rich and influential people, who at the instigation of the evil crowned rider of the white horse, have brought misery to humanity and martyrdom to many believers.

The wrath that overtakes them is spoken of in terms of *a great earthquake.* Seismic phenomena were common in the region of proconsular Asia, as we have seen, and the imagery will have been very meaningful to John's readers. It must have been common for them to *hide in caves and among the rocks of the mountains.* Perhaps, too, John also calls to mind the eruption of Vesuvius a decade and a half earlier (AD 79) when the two Italian cities of Pompeii and Herculaneum were buried under volcanic ash. Pliny's description of this disaster from a ship in the Bay of Naples (Book vi, *Epistles* 16,20) could well match John's words that *the sun turned black . . . and the moon blood red . . . and every mountain and island was removed from its place.* Pliny describes the immense quantity of pumice and ash which fell from the sky and so obliterated the sun from view that it was quite dark even in daytime. Doubtless the amazing events at Vesuvius were known all over the world, including by John and his readers.

(4)   The interlude: first part (7:1–8)

Now follows the interlude, in two parts, which portrays the peace and protection of those who have suffered so much at the hands of the tyrant and his assistants.

The destruction which is to come on *the land and sea* is not to injure *the servants of God*, on whose *foreheads . . . a seal* is to be placed. God's angels protect them.

These are the *one hundred and forty four thousand, twelve thousand* being taken from each of the twelve tribes of Israel. This represents the faithful ones from the old covenant, the true Jews as John would call them (2:9; 3:9). This number, like others in the Revelation, is symbolic not literal. If this number is to be taken literally then so must others. But, as we have suggested elsewhere, to ignore the symbolism of the Revelation is to destroy its message and to invite weird interpretations. The point John is making here is that godly Hebrews under the old covenant enjoy the eternal protection of God and are at no disadvantage compared to believers under the new covenant.

(5)   The interlude: second part (7:9–17)

As the great finale to this sequence John again sees the throne, the One seated on the throne and the Lamb. Before these stand an innumerable multitude of people taken, not merely from the Jewish people but from *every nation, tribe, people, and language* (v.9). Their white robes and palm branches both symbolize their victory over opposition and adversity and their fidelity to the Lamb.

Once again we encounter the two-beat rhythm of evangelical declaration and worshipful response. Thus the great multitude declares that *salvation belongs to our God . . . and to the Lamb* (v.10). Well do they understand that. They have come out of *the great tribulation*, that is, the grim epoch which has been marked by tyranny, persecution and martyrdom. They know from the pain of their sufferings that salvation is found only in their God. It is only by the *blood of the Lamb* that they triumph, that their *robes* are *white*.

Angels, elders and living creatures acknowledge the truth of this and reply in worship that *praise . . . glory . . . wisdom . . . thanks . . . honour . . . power . . . strength be to our God* (v.12). Worship, we again note, is the heart-felt affirmation about God in response to the declaration of the gospel.

In contrast to the great ordeal from which they have emerged there awaits them the presence and protection of their God and of the Lamb. God will *spread his tent over them* and they will not suffer again the *hunger, thirst* or exposure to scorching heat they experienced at the hands of the tyrants. He will *wipe every* suffering *tear from their eye*. The Lamb will *shepherd* them (an evoca-tive paradox), and *will lead them to springs of living water*.

The horrors of the great tribulation, as depicted by the six seals, which would have been immediately understood by John's readers, are followed by the quietness and goodness of life in the presence and under the protection of God. As we will see, much of this description will be repeated in the final chapters when John speaks about the New Jerusalem.

QUESTIONS ON REVELATION CHAPTERS 6–7.

1. What do the four horses and riders represent and what is the relationship between them? How should Christians in Germany during World War II or in Beijing in June 1989, have understood this imagery? What should it mean for us now?

2. What messages are there for us in the reply to the martyrs (6:9–11)?

3. How do we see God's controlling hand even in problems described? See 6:1–8; 7:3.

4. How might John's readers have found encouragement in 7:11–17? How should we find encouragement in this today?

5. What are the two main elements in the words of 7:10–12 and how do they bear on our worship?

Chaos 8–11

(1)   The seventh seal: silence in heaven (8:1-5)

The seventh seal serves as a bridge into the next sequel. Thus John sees *seven angels* with *seven trumpets* (8:2). These trumpets herald the judgment of God on the world which he has created but which has rejected him. The trumpets are only blown, however, after a period of *silence* and the ascent of *the prayers of the saints.* Although these prayers appear futile on earth they are the prelude to the outpouring of *thunder* and *lightning* from heaven which mark the beginning of the judgments which follow.

It may be thought that what follows is extreme, out of touch, unrealistic. As we read it the question is raised within our minds: what is our life, our existence, really like? Is it dark or sunny? For some periods the great painter Van Gogh would paint the sunny, bright scenes for which he is famous. But in between these times his paintings were dark, almost black, portraying suffering and despair. Clearly he experienced life as both brightness and darkness. The Revelation, both here and elsewhere, paints life on earth in darkened hues. It does not view life in a romantic way. Nonetheless it is not a counsel of despair; ultimately it is a message of hope. Although apocalyptic in style it depicts life within history with both realism and insight.

(2) *The first four trumpets: cosmic chaos (8:6–12)*

The chaos depicted here is in contrast to the serene, "good" heavens and earth created by God described in Genesis 1. But Genesis 1 was a world in which humanity, as God's image, was to exercise a thankful dominion over all things as God's representative on earth. Soon, however, human ingratitude, rebellion and outright disobedience led God to drive people out of the Garden. Thus people now inhabit a world whose fabric is subject to profoundly destructive forces. Men and women do not live in Eden, in paradise.

As the trumpets sound in turn, the various parts of the cosmos are bombarded. Terrifying destruction is hurled down or at *earth . . . trees . . . grass . . . sea . . . rivers . . . waters . . . sun . . . moon . . . stars.* Some of the vocabulary used in Exodus to describe the plagues (for example hail and blood cf 9:22) is used by John. As in the sequence about tyranny we find that cinematic images tend to confirm John's apocalyptic images.

Through newsreel and television film we see awesome cyclones, torrential flooding, engulfing mudslides, storm-driven, mountainous seas, surging volcanic lava, and fiercely raging bushfires. The "forces of nature" unleashed in the world sometimes assume apocalyptic proportions. Men and women in John's time were even more helpless in the face of earthquakes, volcanoes and cyclones than we are. We, at least, sometimes have early warnings and some mechanisms for disaster relief. Nonetheless, when the heavens rage and the earth moves we have no strength to fight these great forces. We may only take shelter as best we are able, until they pass.

Despite their severity these events are not *the* end the cosmos. *One third* is destroyed, to be sure, but not three thirds. (Symbolically, the numbers mean "many, but not a majority".) For when three thirds are destroyed that will indeed be the end. Trumpet-like, these outpoured horrors herald the end. They speak of wrath poured out into a world where men and women have rejected God. This is wrath within history, partially revealed, which points to a wrath to be completely revealed at the end of history. But these terrors also speak of God's (severe) mercy; two thirds of the cosmos are spared.

But trumpets five, six and seven signal the coming of even worse judgments, which will befall, not the physical frame of the cosmos, but its chief inhabitant, mankind. Thus the high flying eagle with panoramic view of the world utters the threefold "woe" to *the inhabitants of the earth*.

(3)   Trumpet five: the torture of mankind (9:1–11)

The fifth trumpet signals the *spiritual* torture, as opposed to the physical sufferings, experienced by mankind. The source of this suffering is Satan who is called "destroyer" (Hebrew: *Abaddon*; Greek: *Apollyon*), the *angel of the abyss*. The *fallen . . . star* which was given *the key* to open the abyss is not identified (9:1). It is probably no more significant in itself than the other objects hurled at the cosmos in chapter nine. In writing of the smoke that rose as from a gigantic furnace causing sun and sky to be darkened John is likening the now-opened abyss to a volcano. It is unlikely that John is directly prophesying the nuclear holocaust.

From the depths of the Abyss arise myriads of dreadful locusts whose *sting, like that of . . . the scorpion*, brought such *agony* that people *seek . . . , but will not find . . . , death* (9:6). Abaddon/Apollyon is king over these stinging creatures (9:11).

Those *tormented* do not have *the seal of God on their foreheads* (9:4). In other words, Satan is afflicting those who obey and worship him. They suffer for *five months* which is taken to mean a period within history. It is worth being reminded that Satan is not only the accuser of God's people; he is also the tormenter of his own. The man named "Legion" lived in tortured solitude, crying out throughout the night from the eerie tombs. Yet he knew within himself that all was not well. He was a torn, driven man; a tormented man (Mark 5:1–20). Satan truly is a destroyer.

The First Letter of John declares that "the whole world is under the control of the Evil One" (5:19). This must mean that, to some degree or another, all people are afflicted and tormented by "the angel of the abyss". When men and women deliberately turn their backs on God and walk towards Satan, they place themselves in the hands of a tormenter, not a friend. Modern European society has rejected the active expression of the Christian faith. The churches are but poorly attended. Many remain passive or nominal Christians, with whom there is still some intellectual assent to Christian beliefs. But many others have moved to alternative belief systems, including the occult. It has been claimed that there are more witch doctors in France than medical doctors.

The first woe (9.12) for Man is the Satanic torture he experiences. The first four trumpets herald natural disasters; the fifth, satanically-inspired supernatural disasters.

(4)   Trumpet six: the killing of mankind (9:13–21)

The prayers of God's people once more appear to be in mind as somehow precipitating the judgments which will occur on earth. (Prayer had been associated with the *golden altar before God/the throne* in the earlier reference of 8:3).

The sixth trumpet call was followed by a voice speaking, surely the voice of God, in response to the prayers of the people. Once more we note that though it appears weak and ineffectual, prayer is is fact powerful.

In consequence, *four angels* who had been *bound at the ... River Euphrates* are released (9:14). The Euphrates was the home of the dreaded Parthians whose hordes of galloping cavalry, it was feared, would engulf the Roman Empire. Nonetheless, these awful charging cavalry as described by John are no foreign invader, but the armies of Satan, come not to torment but to kill. These horses, symbolically described, come from the four evil angels; they kill with mouth and tail. Their numbers, given symbolically as *two hundred million* (9:16), are really beyond calculation.

Again cinematic images converge with apocalyptic: skeletons at Belsen, starved, stick-like children in Ethiopia, car-bombed victims in Beirut and Belfast. Television stations sometimes soften the impact of the disasters they report by concluding their news telecasts with a reassuring, lighthearted or happy-ever-after story. They who bring us the news to some extent portray themselves as God-like, as somehow in control of an out-of-control world.

Despite the horrors described by John, however, the end is not yet. Many from within mankind are violently killed, symbolically represented as *a third* (9.15). The greater majority, however, are spared. Will they understand that these evils are but portents of a coming judgment which will engulf all? Will they now turn back to God?

Part of the message for us is that people cannot create paradise on earth. Certainly we should seek early meteorological and seismic warning of natural disasters and take every prudent step to improve health and educational services. Mankind never seems to learn, however, that there is no uniform progress towards Utopia. Progress and regress appear to exist side by side at every point in history including within our own times. The principle and power of corruption and evil appear to be ineradicable from history and society. Mankind is incapable of building heaven on earth. The New Jerusalem does not arise out of the old; it descends from heaven as God's gift.

John comments, with more than a suggestion of sadness, that those who were not killed *still did not repent of worshipping demons* or the idols made by their own hands, blind, deaf and immobile though they are (9:20). Satan is, of course, the god standing behind the demons and the gods worshipped by these people. Even though he torments and kills them, they continue to bow down before him. Nor is there any turning from the accompanying evils of *murder, magic arts, sexual immorality, or theft* (9:21).

It is not, however, that John expects that mankind will simply turn from idolatry, demons and ungodly behaviour on account of the plagues that befall them. The plagues of themselves do not point away from Abaddon/Apollyon to God. What is needed is prophecy, the word of God, to explain and interpret to mankind that the plagues give warning of a coming, eternal wrath, which will fall on everybody. Prophecy will also extend to the hearers deliverance from sins and the power of darkness through the blood of Jesus. It is to the matter of prophecy that the Revelation now turns as it leaves behind the sixth trumpet and enters the interlude before the seventh trumpet.

(5)   Interlude (a): the call to prophesy (10:1–11)

The *mighty angel* John sees is holding *a little scroll* which lays *open in his hand*. His towering stature as God's intermediary is in contrast to the perception that the cause of Christ on earth is pitiful and ineffectual. The new sequence of seven thunders which is about to begin at his shout is broken off; no more is heard of it (10:4).

This massive angel who overarches land, sea and sky, *swore* by the name of God that there is to be *no more delay* and that the sounding of the *seventh ... trumpet* will reveal at last the *mystery of God* (9:6–7). God's *servants, the* (New Testament) *prophets*, already know this mystery, but will they declare it in the midst of a world which is marked by tyranny, martyrdom and chaos? Will the prophets be brave enough to speak the word of God and the testimony of Jesus at a time of such suffering and danger for them? Surely being exiled on bleak Patmos is bad enough? Why should John invite further pain or even death?

John then hears *the voice* of Jesus (10:8 cf 4:1; 1:10) summoning him to take the scroll from the hand of the mighty angel. This is a renewed commissioning of John. The *scroll will turn* his *stomach sour* but *it will be as sweet as honey* in his mouth. Here is the great insight that prophecy is bitter *and* sweet, painful *and* pleasurable. The question is: will John (and others among his readers) take the scroll and speak that prophetic word to men and women in a cosmos surrounded by chaos, torment and death?

In obedience to Jesus' command John took the scroll and ate it, that is, he digested the prophetic word that God directs to people. It should be noted that while prophecy in the Old Testament was directed to Israel, New Testament prophecy is *about many peoples, nations, languages and kings* (10:11). Prophecy, which is the word of God and the testimony of Jesus, is now for all peoples in the cosmos created by God, not only for Israel. Prophecy is God's word, the gospel, directed to men and women living in a cosmos in chaos. And in this John was God's obedient servant, despite the scroll's bitterness to his stomach. Here is great challenge for us.

(6)   Interlude (b): the deaths of the two prophets (11:1–14)

We now see why the message of the prophet is bitter. Two prophets are killed in the streets of the city where they are prophesying. Clearly it is dangerous and painful to be a prophet.

But who are these two prophets and what is the city in which they met their deaths? John is both allusive and elusive in what he now writes, perhaps to throw would-be persecutors off the scent. We assume that his original readers knew what he was referring to, even if we have some difficulty.

The city in verses 1–6 appears to be Jerusalem; it is called the *holy city* (v.2). John thinks of it in two separate parts as: (i) the *temple of God, altar, worshippers* and (ii) the *outer court* and the *Gentiles.*

John is to *measure* the temple and altar and *count* the worshippers, that is, protect and preserve these for heaven. Chapter 11 concludes by stating *then God's temple in heaven was opened.* God's holy place is no longer on earth, but in heaven, as Jesus said it would be (see John 2:19–22). Jesus' death and resurrection spelt the end of the great earthly shrine in Jerusalem. No longer would there be a holy place on earth for God's people to gather. Believers now gather by faith in the temple in heaven, in the presence of the Enthroned One and the Lamb who was slain for their sins. As we come to the final two chapters we discover that the new temple is the New Jerusalem, the City of God which is to come down from heaven.

The outer court, that is, the remainder of historical Jerusalem, is not to be measured. It is to be *given* to the *Gentiles* who will trample on it for *forty two months* or three and a half years, a long but not unlimited historical period. John is here alluding to the Romans' destruction of Jerusalem and its temple a quarter of a century earlier, in AD 70. Vivid eye-witness descriptions of these events have survived in Josephus' great work *The Jewish War*, which the reader is encouraged to consult (see the Penguin edition).

Jerusalem as an earthly city has no ongoing place in the purposes of God. Apart from its interest to historians, archaeologists and tourists Jerusalem has no further theological significance. It did not receive its long-awaited king when he came; Jerusalem was the city in which the *Lord was crucified* (11:8).

With stunning and calculated inconsistency John calls the holy city *Sodom and Egypt* (11:8). By its killing of Jesus Jerusalem has proved just as pagan and hostile to God's people as Sodom and Egypt had been. John probably also has in mind other cities in more recent times where God's servants have been rejected–places like Rome where Peter and Paul and many others were killed in AD 64–65. Perhaps he is also thinking of the cities of proconsular Asia like Pergamum where persecution has now broken out because Christians will not participate in the emperor-cult.

The *great city* in which prophecy is declared does not refer to one specific city. It represents any metropolis hostile to the word of God, whether Jerusalem, Rome, Ephesus, Smyrna or Pergamum.

Likewise the *two witnesses* (11:3) stand for those individuals or churches (*lampstands* 11:4) who prophesy faithfully in their cities. The duration of the period in which they will prophesy is also three and a half years (*1260 days* 11:3), a lengthy but not eternal span.

The *power* Christ *will give* to his *two witnesses* is as for the *two olive trees* (11:4). This is evocative of Zechariah chapter four where it is stated that God's will is achieved: ' "not by power, nor by might but by my Spirit", says the Lord' (4:6). For the time of their prophecy they will enjoy the protection from God *from anyone who tries to harm them* (11.5), though exactly what this entails is not clear to us. As with the prophets Elijah and Moses from the old covenant these prophets *will have power*, respectively, *to shut up the sky so that it will not rain* and . . . *to strike the earth with every kind of plague* (11:6). Again, we have difficulty penetrating the symbolism to know what John intended his original readers to understand. Quite possibly he is referring to the potent effects of prayer, as mentioned earlier, as a prelude to the outpouring of God's judgments on the earth (cf 8:4–5; 9:13).

Eventually, however, the "Destroyer" from the abyss, Abaddon/Apollyon, *will attack . . . overpower and kill them* (v.7). In their apparent helplessness *their bodies will lie in the street of the great city . . . and men . . . will refuse them burial* (v.10). The deaths of the prophets will result in gloating and celebration by *the inhabitants of the earth*. These details may refer to nothing in particular, or, they could perhaps speak of the specific circumstances of the deaths of some contemporary martyrs which John's readers will understand, but which we today do not.

The bizarre reference to the resurrection and ascension of these martyred prophets after three and a half days probably points to their participation in the first resurrection, that is in the resurrection of Jesus (cf 20:4). They have emerged victorious from the great tribulation in which they have lost their lives.

According to John *a tenth of that city collapsed* as a result of a *severe earthquake* (v.13). Once again John may be appealing to local knowledge of the circumstances surrounding the martyrdom of local believers. Perhaps their deaths were accompanied by an earthquake in that city. (Certainly earthquakes were very common in proconsular Asia.) It may be that the coincidence of the earthquake with the deaths of the prophets provoked *terror* in the citizens and the giving of *glory to the God of heaven.*

(7)   The seventh trumpet (11:15–19)

Now at last the seventh trumpet is to be sounded. The mystery of God, long hidden, will now be revealed. There is no more delay (cf 10.6).

It is a mystery which could never have been guessed at, for it has been revealed not at the end of all things but in the midst of all things. This mystery has been revealed during, not at the conclusion of, the chaos in the cosmos. It has happened while God is bombarding the earth, while the hordes of *Abaddon/Apollyon* torment humanity, while the fiendish horses destroy a third of humanity. What is this mystery ?

As the trumpet is sounded, loud voices in heaven call out:

*The kingdom of the world and **has become***
the kingdom of our Lord and of his Christ
he will reign for ever and ever (v15).

This statement is equivalent to that made earlier, namely that the Lion of the tribe of Judah **has conquered**. As we saw this referred to the sacrificial and redemptive death of the Lamb (5:5–6). The conquest of the Lion and the now-arrived Kingdom of God are present realities based on past events. This is the witness that cost the two prophets their lives, the bitter/sweet message which John shrinks from declaring, but which the world in its pain needs to hear and believe. It is not the message of a still-to-come, last battle. Rather it is the message of Lamb that was slain to liberate men and women from their sins and from the power of evil. It tells of a battle fought and a victory won.

This great evangelical utterance is answered in thanksgiving by the twenty four elders:

We give thanks to you, Lord God Almighty . . .
because you have taken your great power
and begun to reign (v17).

The reign of God does not lie in the future. It is indeed a present reality based on the great saving events of the first Easter.

This is the source of the present conflict between the Roman Imperial authorities and the people of God. Because God has begun to reign in the lives of people, *the nations were angry* . . . with God *and* his people. The deaths of the prophets and the persecution of the people arises from the anger of the nations.

All the end-time events flow on from the Lion-Lamb's eschatological (that is, relating to the end times) victory within history. God's *wrath has come* and will yet come in *judging the dead*, in *rewarding prophets* and *saints* and in *destroying those who destroy the earth*. The various sequences in John's book prophesy the occurrence of these things both within and at the end of history. The first Easter was the planting of seed, which has been growing since and which will reach its appointed harvest at the right time.

QUESTIONS ON REVELATION CHAPTERS 8–11.

1. Consider carefully the scale and extent of destruction in 8:6–12. How does it relate to (a) the order and goodness described in Genesis 1 and 2, and (b) the flood in Genesis 7–9?

2. What purpose is behind such destruction?

3. Who are the objects of Satan's torture in 9:1–11? What insight does this give us into his real nature and power of deception?

4. What is John's prophetic word (11:7–10,15)? What made it "sour"? Does it remain just as sour today?

5. Why were the nations angry at the message (11:16–18)? What equivalent responses do we face today, individually and as a church? What is the real focus of such anger?

15

Persecution 12–14

These chapters relating to persecution are critical within the structure of the Revelation. They arise out of the sufferings of Christians in the cities of proconsular Asia as described in chapters 2 and 3. But they also point forward to the overthrow of the persecutors in chapters 18–20. It is appropriate that John has located them so centrally in his book; they tie the whole together.

Chapters 12–14, however, could almost be regarded as a self-contained or free-standing tract, able to be considered on its own. One major theme presents a brief history of Christianity from the birth of Jesus [in Judaea] to the outbreak of persecution against his people [in proconsular Asia]. It refers to the birth of the Christ-child, the attempt of evil King Herod to destroy him and the escape of the child to heaven. There follows an account of the Jews' unsuccessful pursuit of the Jerusalem church to the wilderness [of Transjordan in the middle 60s]. Finally, to bring things up to date, John describes how persecution has now spread from Judaea to the place for which his book is being written, proconsular Asia. Our author has written a mini-history of early Christianity covering a historical span of 100 years.

The other great theme running through this sequel of scenes is the message of the prophetic word, the gospel, the testimony of Jesus. There comes before us the male child, the Lamb whose blood was shed and who was snatched up to heaven, from which he rules the nations as God's anointed king. Salvation and the kingdom of God have now come in the great victory of the Lamb's death and resurrection/ascension. As for the future, on one hand, the Lamb and his faithful people are safe on Mount Zion, while, on the other hand, those who have persecuted them are called on to "fear God and give him glory" in view of the coming judgment. This latter proclamation is called the "eternal gospel", even though it is a message of doom to those who reject the Lamb and his people.

John appears to have three aims in writing these chapters. First, he shows his readers that the oppression they are experiencing is of Satanic origin. Their struggle is not merely against "flesh and blood", merely against local Roman and Asian officials nor even against the Emperor Domitian. They are resisting the Devil himself, no less.

Second, his suffering readers need to know that the Devil's time is short and that he, his beast-like agents, and his community of supporters will soon be overthrown and destroyed.

Third, John calls his readers patiently to endure their sufferings, in loyalty to Jesus. He does not shield them from the grim probability that faithfulness to Jesus in the face of the emperor-cult will mean captivity and death. Being a Christian is a life and death commitment in the face of an implacable and determined enemy which had absolute confidence in the rightness of its rule. It could be said that a state of war existed between the Devil and his earthly agents against the Lamb and his people.

Unlike the earlier sequences of scenes there are no symbols used in this sequence. John does use the word *sign* on a number of occasions (Greek: *semeion*, 12:1,3; 13:13,14) but these are not numbered like the seals or the trumpets. Nonetheless, the familiar structure of six scenes, an interlude and a seventh scene may be discerned. Like the other sequences of scenes, however, this sequence is concurrent with the others, not consecutive.

(1)   The woman, the male child and the dragon (12:1-6)

Who is the *woman* in Revelation 12? As we have seen already John is calculatedly inconsistent in his use of his images. In the first part of the chapter she appears to be identified with Mary the mother about to give birth to her male child Jesus. Perhaps Mary is seen as part of that pious remnant of Jews, represented by Simeon and Anna, among whom the Messiah was born and nurtured. But in the latter part of the chapter the identity of the woman is changed. Now she is the fleeing Jerusalem church, seventy years later. The common element is that the "woman" in both cases is a suffering person, and in that sense can be said to represent the persecuted church of the Lamb.

That she is **in heaven** ... *clothed with the sun, with the* **moon** *under her feet* is suggestive of her ultimate triumph and her *crown of twelve stars* symbolises the community of the redeemed. In all probability this woman is also to be identified with the heavenly, beautifully dressed bride who descends from heaven for her marriage with the Lamb referred to in Chapter 21.

The woman's *son, her male child, who will rule all the nations with an iron sceptre,* clearly is Jesus (cf 19:15; Psalm 2:9). (An earlier reference, however, shows that

Jesus' rule over the nations will be shared by his faithful people. See 2:27). Who is the historical person, as symbolised by the dragon, who menaces the child-messiah? The attempt by evil King Herod to destroy the one whom he perceived to be a threat to his rule, even though this person was a baby (Matthew 2:1–18) is probably what John intends us to think. That Herod's action was directed at one already born as opposed to the Revelation's reference to the child not yet born is probably too precise an objection against so creative a writer as John.

The *enormous red dragon* (12:3) is identified as *that ancient serpent called the devil and Satan* (12:9 cf Genesis 3:1–19). His pretentions to divine wisdom and power are implied, respectively, by the *seven* [crowned] **heads and ten horns**.

He is the great, primeval enemy of God who *deceives the nations* (20:3,8,10) and *leads the whole world astray* (12:9) so that people should not worship the true and living God. Instead he deceives people so that they believe divine power is to be found in human rulers.

At that time the Roman Emperor Domitian demanded that his subjects throughout the Empire call him "Lord and God" (Suetonius, *Domitian* 13). Domitian's court poet Statius affectedly refers to his master as " . . . off-spring and sire of mighty deities . . . whose godhead I heard from afar" (*Silvae* I.i.66) and as "ruler of the nations and mighty sire of the conquered world" (*Silvae* IV.ii.11). Satan had deceived and led astray the whole world to believe the lie that the Emperor was God, including the citizens of Roman proconsular Asia. He recognised in advance the threat posed to these pretentious claims by the true Messianic ruler who was to come. Thus he positioned himself in front of the woman as she was about to give birth to the man child, who would become the real ruler of the nations, to kill the child at birth. By these symbols John is teaching that the war in which the Christians in the Asian cities find themselves had its historic beginning in the attack on the Christ-child and its primordial origins in the Serpent's deception of Adam and Eve.

(2)   The dragon is cast down to earth (12:7–12)

The dragon is very determined. Thwarted in his attempts to destroy the woman and the child on earth he pursues the child to heaven where he has been *snatched up to God and to his throne* (v.5). Thus there was *war in heaven* (v.7) as the dragon attacked its very gates. The dragon and his angels lost their place in heaven and were hurled to the earth, not because *Michael and his angels* were stronger (for clearly they were not, v.3), but because of the man child who had been snatched up to God to rule the nations. Christ has won the great victory and he is the ruler of the nations on the basis of his redemptive death. The Lion of the tribe of Judah has conquered as the Lamb that was slain (5:5–6). The events of the first Easter and their significance remain central for John.

Thus John hears a loud voice in heaven say (the speaker is not identified):

*Now **have come** the salvation*
the power
and the kingdom of our God
and the authority of his Christ (12:10).

The snatching up to heaven of the Messiah, in virtue of his redemptive death, coincides with the hurling down to the earth of the great dragon, Satan. We are reminded of Jesus' words as recorded in the Gospel of John: "Now shall the ruler of this world be cast out; and I, when I am lifted up from the earth [in crucifixion/ascension] will

104

draw all men to myself" (John 12:31–32 RSV). It is clear that the words in the Revelation echo the words of Jesus.

The evidence that Christ is now ruling in heaven may be seen in the persecution of his people on earth. John writes "*Now* [has] come . . . the authority of Christ. *For* the accuser of our brothers . . . has been cast down". The heavens may rejoice that the dragon has been cast down; but it is bad news for those who live on earth. He is filled with fury at his loss of power and because he knows that in a short time he will be destroyed (12:12). That the brothers or fellow-Christians in Asia are being accused at that time is sure proof that Christ has conquered and is ruling. Let the persecuted believers take heart in that fact.

The one group who will not worship the emperor as god, the one people of all the peoples not deceived, not led astray by the Devil are the people loyal to Jesus. (That is, apart from the Jews, who alone were legally relieved of the obligation to participate in the emperor-cult). Hence the dragon *accuses them night and day before our God* (v.10), words evoking a picture of Christians accused before Roman magistrates or Asian priests of treason, of disloyalty to the state and ingratitude to the emperor. Perhaps the Jews, who enjoyed imperial protection in cultic matters, but who were hostile to Christians as a heretical and schismatic sect, had reported them to the authorities (cf 2:9; 3:9). The dragon is illiberal, intolerant of nonconformity. All must worship the Emperor. The resistance of Christians in this situation and on subsequent occasions in history has contributed significantly to one of the great and cherished rights in free, democratic societies: the right to assemble and worship in freedom. Christians must ensure that other groups enjoy the same freedom.

Despite the determined hostility of the dragon in his continuing warfare against God and his people, he may be defeated. He is not invincible, despite his enormous wisdom and power. John writes that these incessantly accused ones *overcame* (*enikesan*) him (12:11). The same verb *nikan* in the same aorist tense (signifying completed action) is used of the Lion of the tribe of Judah who has triumphed (*enikesen*: 5:5). Christ's victory and his people's victory arise from the one source: the shedding of the Lamb's blood. By his blood they are released from their sins (1:5; 5:9) and so have no fear for themselves before God. They are, in fact, priests of God through the Lamb's blood shed for them (1:6; 5:10). Hence they are unashamed in face of ferocious accusation to speak their word of testimony that they are loyal to Jesus and will not worship Caesar. What can death do to them? We can see why Roman provincial governors of the time came to regard the Christians as characterised by "hatred of the human race" (Tacitus) and "obstinate ... perverse ... unbending" (Pliny).

(3)   *The flight of the woman (12:13–17)*

Cast down from heaven, in consequence of the child being caught up to God, the dragon continued his pursuit of the woman. Her identity is changed to the "mother" church of Christendom, the Church of Jerusalem (cf Galatians 4:26). During the Jewish-Roman war in the 60s the Jerusalem Church fled from the war zone to the safety of Transjordan, to Pella, a city of the Decapolis. This is probably what is intended by *the place prepared for her in the desert* to which she had escaped by *the two wings of the great eagle* and where she *remained out of the serpent's reach* (12:14). Perhaps verses 15–16 refer to a flood in the Jordan valley from which the fugitive

106

church narrowly escaped, but of which we have no independent record.

Now utterly frustrated, the dragon went off *to make war* against the rest of the woman's *offspring*, that is, to believers in other countries, including proconsular Asia, who owe their origin to the Jerusalem Church. If John the author of Revelation is in fact John Zebedee, a former pillar of the Jerusalem Church (Galatians 2:7–9) now migrated to Asia, then his words apply especially to himself.

We see the dragon in an image of implacable hostility standing *on the shore* of the Mediterranean *Sea* looking across the waters to distant lands to which he will pursue and make war against the offspring of the woman. The scene will change immediately to Asia where John will see an awesome beast come out of the sea up on to the land to wage war against the people of Jesus. Clearly the beast is an incarnation of the dragon who stood on the shore in Palestine.

(4)   The beast out of the sea (13:1–10)

The beast that comes out of the sea is a veiled description of Roman imperial power, which owed much of its power to its navy's control of the Mediterranean. Possibly John is describing the arrival by ship of a proconsul in Ephesus, with attendant pomp and ceremony. He represents Roman power and the Roman Imperator and wields full authority in the province to which he has been appointed. He is the embodiment of Roman might and authority among the people of Asia. Doubtless John's descriptions are veiled to escape punishment for treason.

Like the dragon the sea-beast has *seven heads and ten horns*, signifying pretentions to divinity. In his case, unlike the dragon, the ten horns are crowned, signifying perhaps his preoccupation with power as opposed to wisdom. That *one of the heads . . . seemed to have a fatal wound* is often taken to refer to Nero's unsuccessful attempted suicide. (Nero as the first persecuting emperor is thus the sea-beast par excellence). But it should also be noted that just as the true Messiah is the Lamb with a death-wound so the false-Messiah, the anti- (= substitute) Christ, also has a wound. By pointing to elements in the bogus ruler (ie. a fatal wound) John is perhaps underscoring the reality of Jesus as the true ruler of the nations and of the kings of the earth.

People's worship of the sea-beast is on account of his invincible power. *"Who is like the beast?"*, they ask. *"Who can make war against him?"* In the period immediately before the outbreak of war in Judaea, according to the Jewish historian Josephus writing in the 70s, the younger Agrippa spoke to the crowds of Jews in Jerusalem pleading with them not to go to war with the Romans. In his long speech he gives a historical survey of nation after nation which has fallen to Roman arms. He speaks grimly of the utterly irresistible power of the Romans. No country on earth, not even the redoubtable Parthians, dare resist them for a moment (*Jewish War* ii, 345–401).

Thus the *beast*, Rome, *is given authority* (by the Dragon) *over every tribe, people, language and nation* (v.7). *All inhabitants of the earth will worship the beast* . . . except, that is, those who belong to the Lamb (v.8). They alone resist the awesome might of the Roman Beast and refuse to worship it. Worship of Satan and of his incarnation Rome, therefore, was worship of naked power. But this has been true of every other totalitarian regime which has regarded itself as the object of human worship and unquestioning obedience.

The *proud words* and *blasphemies* uttered by the beast probably refer to the Emperor Domitian's demand to be worshipped as a divine figure. Dio Cassius wrote that: "Domitian even insisted on being considered a god and was exceedingly proud of being called 'master' (*dominus*) and 'god' (*deus*)" (*Roman History* LXVII,v.7). Domitian was a persecutor also of Jews and of those who followed the Stoic philosophy. In the end he was assassinated by his own household servant. The Roman Senate declared his name to be "of damned memory" and his name was effaced on public monuments and inscriptions. The younger Pliny wrote of him as a "fearful monster [who] built his defences with untold terrors, where lurking in his den he licked up the blood of murdered relatives or emerged to plot the massacre and destruction of his most distinguished subjects. Menaces and horrors were the sentinels at his doors" (*Panegyricus* 48). Even allowing for Pliny's rhetorical excesses it is clear that Domitian was a very cruel and autocratic tyrant.

So much, then, for the self-styled "god" who sought to brutalize believers in Asia to renounce their Lord in acknowledgement of him. It was Domitian *who opened his mouth to blaspheme God and to slander his name and his dwelling place* (13:6). Domitian's provincial represen-tative *was given power* (ie. by the dragon) *to make war against the saints and to conquer them* (13:7). The devil's war against God was expressed first as war against the Messiah-child, then against the Messiah-enthroned, then against the woman and finally against her offspring (12:4,7,17; 13:7). The satanic progression is: war against God, war against Christ, war against Christians.

John makes no pious or romantically triumphalist promises to his suffering readers in Asia. Some believers (like John himself) *will go into captivity*, others (like Antipas: 2:13) will be *killed with the sword* (13:9–10; cf 6:9–11). John gives no offer of miraculous escape from these dire circumstances. Rather, he writes, *this calls for patient endurance and faithfulness on the part of the saints* (13:10). It is by these Christ-like qualities, as displayed by the Lamb in his hour of death, that they will be victorious against the massive forces of Roman imperialism which are pitted against them. In bearing their testimony to Jesus they must not shrink from death.

(5)   The beast out of the earth (13:11–18)

We are now introduced to a second beast whom John describes as *coming out of the earth*. Who is this beast? It is clear that this beast symbolizes the High Priest of proconsular Asia. This high priest was an Asian dignitary who presided over the annual General Assembly of the cities of Asia and officiated in the ceremonies of the Emperor Cult. Although this was a person of high distinction, he has only *two horns* signifying the weakness of the local Asian officials relative to the power of Rome. Nonetheless, *he spoke like a dragon*, that is, in ferocious accusation of the brothers.

The high priest of Asia was responsible for the Asians' participation in the cultic worship of Rome. Nothing could be more important than to ensure the complete loyalty of these Asian provincials to the great power of Rome. He was under considerable pressure, therefore, to ensure that this occurred. The obstinacy of Christians could have reflected badly on his competence as high priest. John's symbolism is very thinly veiled in his description of this beast: *he exercised all the authority of the first beast on its behalf and made its inhabitants worship the first beast, whose fatal wound had been healed* (v.12). It was the role of this beast, the High Priest of Asia, to make the local inhabitants worship the first beast, the Roman Emperor, in acknowledgement of the power and authority of the Empire.

Two of his methods are now described. First, John mentions magical tricks associated with *an image in honour of the beast*. This may be in reference to a five metre high statue of Domitian which had been placed adjacent to a newly erected temple in Ephesus. The remains of the temple are still to be seen in Ephesus and the head of the emperor's statue is displayed in the museum in nearby Selcuk . It is possible that representatives from the whole province gathered in Ephesus for the dedicatory ceremonies. The High Priest made *fire come down from heaven in full view of men* (13:13) and somehow caused *the image* of the emperor *to speak* (13:15). While we do not know by what means these things were done, the practice of sleight of hand and trickery by pagan priests to overawe the gullible was common in antiquity. The effect on those who witnessed these great things on this occasion was to *cause all who refused to worship the beast to be killed* (v.15), perhaps by mob violence. We can detect in John's words, even at this distance in time, something of the pressure which those Christians then felt.

Second, the high priest took some action, whose details are only darkly hinted at here, by which financial sanctions were applied to those who were unwilling to participate in the emperor cult. What is the *mark* on *right hand* and *forehead* that everyone was forced to bear so that *no one could buy or sell* without that mark? Possibly the high priest, in consultation with the proconsul, had instituted a certificate or token for those who had participated in the cultic worship, which could be produced on demand, and without which it was not possible to transact any business. Whatever the precise mechanism used at the time it is clear that the Christians of Asia were now in a position of grave personal disadvantage.

Ultimately, this mark, whatever it actually was, is the *name* or *number* of the beast. Doubtless for reasons of security, John does not give the name of the Roman emperor. He does, however, give his number, 666. As it was not possible to write numerals in Hebrew and Greek, writers in those languages were forced to use letters of their alphabets to denote numbers. Thus a=1, b=2 and so on. But it is almost impossible to be sure what letters are intended by John's six hundred and sixty six, though there have been many guesses. It is not even certain whether we are to seek an answer in Hebrew or Greek! The most favoured speculation is that 666 = Nero Caesar [in Hebrew, more or less!]. This emperor, it will be remembered, was the first persecutor, a larger than life figure among emperors in the recent half century and one, furthermore, whom many expected to come back from the dead and resume his former position.

More certain, however, is the significance of the numbers. The dragon and the sea beast each have seven heads (12:3; 13:1); they present themselves a divinely wise. But seven is God's number, eternal and divine; six is merely human, *man's number*. In this context six is an evil and pretentious approximation; triple six perhaps represents the evil trinity of the dragon, the sea beast and the land beast, posturing as God.

Fascinating though John's 13th chapter is as a historical commentary on the political and religious pressure being applied to Christian believers in proconsular Asia in the nineties, its significance extends far beyond its original context. His words show that a secular ruler's demand to be worshipped/obeyed without question, as supported by religion or ideology, will mean great conflict for Christians. It does not matter whether it is Stalin, Hitler or the emperor of Japan, the principle will hold true.

Christians are to render to Caesar civil obedience, the payment of taxes and reasonable cooperation. But they may not worship Caesar, only God. Whenever Caesar, in whatever historical dress he appears, demands worship of his subjects, then he has become anti-Christ, substitute Christ. Those Christians fortunate enough to live under democratic rule should be very thankful indeed for this providence and, at the same time, deeply prayerful for those of our family who live under regimes where they are brought into dangerous conflict with the authorities.

John issues two calls to his readers in chapter 13, trapped as they were by the evil alliance of the sea beast and the land beast. One call is for *patient endurance and faithfulness* (13:10) in the face of what is, in reality, Satanic assault. The devil's war against Christ is expressed as war against his people. They, like their Lamb-leader, do not shrink from death (12:11).

John's second call to his readers is for *wisdom* (13:18) to understand that the forces pitted against them are neither divine nor eternal. Despite his pretensions to deity, as signified by his seven heads, the beast's number is a human number. In other words, while the evil one who inspires this assault is a supernatural being, his human instrument is not. Wisdom, as mediated by John's teaching, will enable the reader to have a true perspective on these matters. The beast is only human.

(6)   The Lamb and the 144,000 (14:1–5)

John now looks away from this scene of war on earth in which Christians are under grievous assault. He looks, and there before him is *Mount Zion*, the Holy City, the New Jerusalem, which will finally descend on and conclude history as we know it (see 21:2).

Standing there, silent but victorious, is *the Lamb* that had been slain but which had been snatched up to God

113

(cf 5:6; 12:5). With him are the *144,000*, a number which earlier symbolized the faithful ones from among the twelve tribes of the Jews (7:4–8) but which now appears to be the complete number of those *redeemed from the earth*, Jews and Gentiles. (John uses his symbols to teach different things in different places; the context must decide the meaning of the symbol). Accompanied by thunderously loud harps they sing *a new song*, a song not known to anybody else except those who have been redeemed. At the great festivals in the cities of Roman Asia hymns of praise to the Emperor were sung; the words of the song of the redeemed on Mount Zion will not be known to those who have worshipped the beast, only to those who have been loyal to the Lamb.

The 144,000 have four qualities. First, they are *redeemed* people. The former slavery implied by that word refers to the power and guilt of sin in which they had been held (1:5; 5:9) and also to their previous submission to Satan through their worship of the gods, including the emperor (13:3–4, 14). Through the blood of the Lamb, however, they have been *purchased* (14:4) and are now free from the grip of those powers.

Second, they have *not defiled themselves with women*. The various temple cults, including the emperor cult, were characterized by sacral prostitution, and John may be referring to this in particular. Clearly, though, his words will relate in general to upholding Christian standards of sexual morality by believers. Unrepented sexual immorality will disqualify us from being numbered with the redeemed.

Third, *they follow the Lamb wherever he goes*. If it is asked, 'Where does the Lamb go?', the answer is that the Lamb goes to death in faithfulness to God. When Jesus was going to Jerusalem to the death he knew awaited him there, he said that his disciples must be prepared to take up a cross, that is, be prepared to die because of their identification with him (Mark 8:34). Being a disciple meant being prepared to lose one's life. John's words here are explained by his earlier comment: *they did not love their lives so much as to shrink from death* (13:11) and *if anyone is to be killed with the sword, with the sword he will be killed* (13:11). A commitment to the Lamb greater than one's fear of death is a prerequisite to being counted among the 144,000. Loyalty to the Lamb in life, however, will mean resurrection at death. Thus those who die faithful to the Lamb are firstfruits, an advanced reaping of the coming eschatological harvest.

Fourth, those who will be with the Lamb on Mount Zion are people of truth, *no lie was found in their mouth; they were blameless.* Possibly the initial reference was to Christians who had not saved their necks by lying to the authorities about their Christian profession. As is usually the case, however, John's words have a more general application.

(7)   The interlude — first part: three angels (14:6–11)

The sequence of scenes relating to persecution is, as we have seen, rich in its references to the gospel. Reference to the male child born to the woman and caught up to God to rule the nations, and also to the Lamb that was slain, while using imagery distinctive to John, nonetheless reminds us of evangelical statements found elsewhere in the apostolic writings.

The messages of the three angels which now follow are also evangelical, but in unexpected ways. Their words are directed to the peoples who follow the (sea) beast and to Babylon, the pagan civilization which has arisen as an alternative to and parallel with God's true purposes for humanity.

The first angel has *an eternal gospel to proclaim to those who live on earth; to every tribe, language and people.* His message is: *the hour of [God's] judgment has come.* The Lion of the tribe of Judah has conquered and is ruling the nations; the dragon has been hurled down. God has passed his judgment on the evil one and on all evil. The whole community of evil ruled by Satan is under the sentence of condemnation, awaiting only the God-ordained moment of execution. This is described later in 14:14–20.

How then, should those who belong to the community of evil respond to this gospel? Because his hour of judgment has come they should *fear God and give him glory . . . worship him who made the heavens, the earth, the sea and the springs of water.* Men and women must turn from worshipping the deification of power as embodied in the emperor; they must repent of bowing down before the man-conceived, hand-made images of stone and gold. Instead they must acknowledge from their hearts their creator, giving him alone glory and worship.

Perhaps it is significant that John writes of an *eternal gospel.* The word "gospel" (Greek: *euaggelion*) was used in an inscription which has been found in a number of cities in proconsular Asia. While it appeared in 9 BC, about a century before John wrote, it had such far reaching effects throughout the whole province that it must have been almost universally known by the people of Asia. Following the demand of the Emperor Augustus the people of Asia abandoned their previous Macedonian calendar and adopted Augustus' birthday (23 September) as their new year's day. This was to express their heartfelt thanks for all the benefits which had come to them from their "saviour", the Emperor Augustus. The inscription states "the birthday of the god (ie. Augustus, 23 September) marked for the world the beginning of good tidings (*euaggelion*) through his coming . . . " (Lewis and Reinhold, *Roman Civilization II*, p64, Harper, 1966).

The poet Virgil wrote of a new, "glorious" age for humanity, the "return of Saturn's reign", "a golden age" having arrived with "a new breed of men sent down from heaven", with the birth of a "boy" child, who is in all probability, Augustus (*Eclogue* IV). Thus the birth of this "god . . . ruler . . . benefactor and saviour . . . of the whole world", as Augustus was also called (Lewis and Reinhold, *op cit*, p64 n.191), was called "gospel".

But this is a secular gospel, a human gospel, whose grotesque message is that a new age has come with a mere human who postures as god, saviour and ruler. This bogus gospel calls on men and women to worship a petty, self-styled god, the Roman emperor. Through the above inscription and other political propaganda the people of Asia would have been familiar with the "gospel of Augustus". John, however, writes not of a secular but of an *eternal* gospel which declares that the age of God's judgment has now arrived and that all must worship the true God. It is not uncommon for 20th century politicians to use "new age" vocabulary of themselves and their party and to clothe themselves in messianic charisma. The Third Reich of Adolph Hitler showed what terrible consequences there are when politicians are allowed to take these claims seriously.

A *second angel* pronounces a further aspect of the eternal gospel, namely that *Babylon the Great*, the city of humanity over against God, is *fallen, fallen*. Because the hour of God's judgment has struck with the death and resurrection of the Lamb, the divine sentence has now been passed against Babylon. Much more will soon appear about Babylon in subsequent chapters of the Revelation. At this stage we should only note that John's reference to Babylon arises out of the building of the city of Babel by the rebellious and unrepentant ones who were descended from those who had been excluded from the garden/paradise (Genesis 11:1–9). In place of Babylon, the city of rebelliousness, will come, by God's gift, the New Jerusalem, which will be nothing less than a new heaven and a new earth (21:1–2).

A *third angel* proclaimed that the *wine of God's fury, the cup of his wrath*, and everlasting torment awaits those who *worship the beast and its image*. Because God has pronounced his judgment on the evil one, the community of evil and all that is opposed to him, we are not surprised that those who worship the beast are under the wrath of God.

We have in the messages of the three angels one message, the eternal gospel, that the hour of God's judgment has now come and that all must repent and turn to him. We may suppose that John's message to unbelievers in Asia bore close similarity to the eternal gospel in its threefold application about which he writes. In other words, not only did John tell them about the Lamb who was slain for their sins, who now ruled the nations and the kings of the earth, he also told them about the doom awaiting those who, in their allegiance to the dragon, refuse to acknowledge the Enthroned One and the Lamb. The eternal gospel, therefore, is a coin with two sides: one positive and the other negative. We seldom mention the negative aspect.

(8)   The interlude — second part: faithfulness (14:12–13)

John makes a further call for faithfulness (cf 13:10). The proclamation of the gospel in both its negative and positive expressions places Christians in a hostile environment, like those in Asia, under enormous pressure.

Those who live are again called to *patient endurance* (Greek: *hypomone*), something John's readers are repeatedly exhorted to show (1:9; 2:2,3,19; 3:10; 13:10). The eternal truth about the Lamb is to be met with immovable steadfastness on the part of his people. John describes *the saints* as those *who obey the commandments of God and remain loyal to Jesus*. This could be regarded as John's definition of a Christian, as one who has submitted to the eternal gospel.

But what are we to think of *the dead who die in the Lord*, those who have been killed in their loyalty to Jesus? John makes various references to these throughout the Revelation. In one place he describes them as safe beneath the altar (6:9) whereas in another, he describes them as reigning with Christ (20:4). There is no contradiction here; both are true. In this passage those who have died faithful to Jesus are pronounced *blessed*. They *rest from their labour* of bearing faithful testimony to Jesus; they are at peace, present with the Lamb on Mount Zion. Moreover, their lost lives are not truly lost, *because their deeds . . . follow them.*

That they have regarded Christ as more important than death cannot fail to make a powerful impact on those who observe their commitment. Who can this person be for whom these people are prepared to die? Would they give their lives for someone who was himself merely a dead martyr? If they back up their "gospel" with a willingness to die for Jesus as the true leader, then perhaps his claims to be ruler should be investigated? In the early church it came to be believed that the "blood of the martyrs was the seed of the church". Great numbers of people found the deaths of Christians to be an irrefutable proof of the truth of the gospel. Their deeds in dying did follow them.

9. *The reaper and the reaping (14:14–20)*

The hour of judgment which came with the death and resurrection of the Lamb is now fulfilled. The picture of the climax of history as a harvest was and remains an apt one. The harvest is the goal, the purpose, the appointed end of the entire agricultural process. God has declared that the story of the world and of mankind has run its appointed course; it is no longer to continue. God sends *an angel* from *the temple*, that is from his own presence, with a command to one *"like a son of man"*, *seated on a white cloud*. God's message through the angel to the one seated on the cloud is *"take your sickle and reap, for the harvest of the earth is ripe"*. As Jesus had taught, it is the Father not the Son who declared when **the** time had finally come (Mark 13:32).

Obedient to the command Jesus *swung the sharp sickle over the earth and the earth was harvested*.

From *the temple*, that is from God himself, emerges *another angel*. Like Jesus, this angel has *a sharp sickle* and at the command of an angel who now comes from the altar, the angel with the sickle gathered up what Jesus had harvested of the earth. The altar, it will be remembered, is the place to which the prayers of the saints ascended (cf 8:3–5). Those prayers, including the cry "how long . . . until you judge the inhabitants of the earth and avenge our blood?" (6:10), appear to have precipitated the judgments of God within history (8:5). Now we infer that these prayers have now precipitated the final command of God through this angel to gather the clusters of grapes from the earth's vine. If Jesus reaped and harvested humanity at the command of God through an angel, then another angel, wielding a sharp sickle at the command of the angel from the altar in response to the prayers of the saints, gathered the grapes into the great winepress.

120

Those who have not repented from idolatry and immorality and come to the Lamb for forgiveness and freedom surely face a dreadful end, according to these words. Here is the *great winepress of the wrath of God* into which the disobedient and ungodly will be cast; their *blood* as high *as a horse's bridle* will flow for hundreds of kilometres. It is clear that John does not wish to be taken literally in this awful picture of judgment. He uses a different picture of the cup of God's wrath and the endless torments of burning sulphur just a few verses earlier (14:10–11). Nonetheless, while we do not take John's picture literally, it is certain that he wishes to be taken seriously. Behind these horrendous images lies the reality that the eternal wrath of God rests on those who reject and oppose him and who make war on his people.

There is a simple truth of the Christian faith which is easy to forget. Jesus taught that his first advent was in mercy, to bring salvation, but that the second advent was for judgment. This is also the consistent teaching of the epistles as well as the gospels. The Revelation focuses on Christ, not as he was in the gospel, bringing salvation, but as he will be, bringing the judgment. It must never be forgotten that the Christ of Revelation, while an encourager and a commender of his people, is an agent of condemnation for those who set themselves against God. This is a hard, difficult to accept teaching, but it is the teaching of Jesus and the Apostles. If the teaching of the Revelation appears harsh let it be remembered that mankind, an ungrateful and rebellious tenant in God's world, has actually shaken its collective fist in the face of God and claimed the ownership for itself. Jesus came to save, but in the absence of repentance and the worship of God, he comes again as judge.

It would be easy enough for the writer to identify the opponents of the Lamb and his people in this sequence as

I have done: Herod, Jewish Zealots, Roman governors and so on. John goes behind the superficially historical identifications to reveal that the real source of this implacable enmity is the ancient serpent, the devil or Satan. Satan is seeking nothing less than the worship of himself as directed towards and through the ruler of the Roman state. From the Roman viewpoint, Christ is an opponent to eliminate and his followers an obstinate, disloyal minority to intimidate and if necessary, eradicate.

John's words were directed in the first instance to suffering believers in the cities of Asia. However, they are applicable to Christians in any situation where the state and its ruler put themselves in the place of God. Such a situation has in fact existed many times in history, including within the century in which we live. For Domitian substitute the names of Hitler or Stalin who set themselves up as God-like beings and demanded total allegiance from their people, and this will be apparent.

QUESTIONS ON REVELATION CHAPTERS 12–14:

1. Why should the dragon seek to kill the male child (12:4)?

2. Read 12:1–6 along with Matthew 1 and 2 to gain, perhaps, a fuller understanding of the 'eternal' dimensions to Jesus' birth.

3. What does the defeat of the dragon in heaven mean for us now (12:7–12)?

4. Why does Satan accuse God's people (12:10)? What effect does this have in our daily lives? How do we best learn the distinction between Satan as accuser and the Holy Spirit as convicter (John 16:8–11)?

5. What are the weapons used by the beast from the sea (13:4–8) and from the earth (13:13–17)?

6. Discuss some modern examples of the alliance of the beast from the sea (political power) and the beast from the earth (false beliefs) against Christians?

7. According to John, who are the 144,000 (14:1–5)?

8. What is the dual message from the angels (14:6–12)? How should this shape our allegiances and desires in modern day "Babylons"?

9. How should the grim description in 14:14–20 shape our lives and witness?

16

Destruction 15–16

We come now to the last of the numbered sequences, a sequence of scenes of the destruction of the world. In an earlier sequence (8–9) John saw and described the partial destruction of the world as created by God. There God was revealing his displeasure within history towards the world community which had rejected him while at the same time restraining and restricting evil and destructive forces. Cinematic images of cyclones, raging oceans, floods, earthquakes, and volcanoes converge with John's apocalyptic scenes.

This sequence is similar to the earlier one, except that the destruction is now total. What is poured out onto the framework of God's creation is now final in its effects.

This sequence is the end of the succession of earlier sequences. The destruction of the present physical world, as depicted in these chapters, is necessary before the coming of the new heavens and the new earth described in the final chapters of the Revelation. These chapters, therefore, represent the end of history and geography as we know them in preparation for God's coming new order.

(1)   Prelude to the end (15:1–8)

John is quite specific. He now sees *the seven last plagues; last, because with them God's wrath is complete* (15:1). We stand looking at the end of the world as we know it.

Before he describes these plagues, however, we see the victorious people of God standing beside the sea. Our minds are taken back to the exodus from Egypt when the Hebrews are on the further, safe side of the Red Sea with their persecutors drowning in the sea behind them. That it is a sea of glass *mixed with fire* speaks of it as God's means of judgment. In later chapters this fiery sea will be the instrument of destruction of the satanic persecutor and his human instruments, the beast and the false prophet (= the beast from the earth).

God's faithful ones, however, are safe. They are identified as *those who had been victorious over the beast and his image and over the number of his name* (15:2). John meant his original readers to see these three things as Satan's weapon used against them at that time: the cult of the Roman emperor, its statues used for worship and his real identity as 666, a man pretending to be God, unmasked. Outside John's immediate situation this means civilization without Christ, civilization opposed to Christ and civilization in the persona of its leader in substitution for Christ. Such a civilization has always imposed great pressure on Christians to bow down before it. To be *victorious* (*tous nikontas* = "those who had conquered" RSV) means to have remained loyal to Jesus regardless of the pain or cost. Christian triumphalism has easily expressed itself as "bigness": big buildings, big congregations, big numbers offering for missionary service. But for John Christian triumph was faithfulness to Jesus in the face of overwhelming odds and great difficulty.

In the previous sequence these faithful ones stand on Mount Zion singing "a new song"; here they stand beside the sea and sing *the song of Moses the servant of God* (the leader of the people under the old covenant) and *the song of the Lamb* (the leader of God's people under the new covenant). John has no doubt that those faithful to God before Christ will be part of the redeemed community; people from both old and new covenant sing one song.

Those who participate in the emperor cult in Roman Asia sing hymns of praise to the pretentious beast-emperor Domitian as "lord and god" and as "ruler of the nations". The song of the faithful-redeemed, however, is addressed to *Lord God Almighty (pantokrator) . . . king of the ages . . . alone holy.* His deeds, in contrast to those of that evil man, are *great and marvellous . . . just and true . . . righteous.* These who sing have no word about themselves or their own heroism in the face of their privations; they sing only of God.

The *eternal gospel* (14:6) had proclaimed that men and women should fear God, give him glory and worship him who created all things. The hour of his impending judgment had come. The singers announce that the hour has indeed arrived and declare to God (15:4) that all nations will come and worship before him. In light of what will soon occur the singers ask: *who will not fear you, O Lord and bring glory to your name?* When God finally reveals himself who will resist him? The outpouring of the plagues that now follow, however, produce no such acknowledgement of God but only cursing of the God of heaven (16:9,10).

John then sees a frightening sight. From the heavenly temple one of the four living creatures gave to seven angels, who had come out of the temple, that is from the presence of God, *seven bowls* (Greek: *phials*) *filled with the wrath of God* (15:7). These are the seven last plagues with which the wrath of God is completed (cf 15:1). None may enter the temple until these plagues are completed.

(2)   *The first six plagues (16:1–12)*

As in chapter eight the first four scenes affect the physical environment in which people live: the earth, the sea, the rivers/springs, the sun. Similarly, scenes five and six affect the principal inhabitant, mankind. In this sequence, however, people are affected by what happens to the earth, the rivers/springs and the sun. Whereas in the earlier sequence there was partial destruction, the destruction is now complete. The plagues remind us, once more, of the plagues against Egypt as described in Exodus. In this chapter John draws extensively on Genesis 1 and Exodus 7–11. Sores, blood, darkness and hailstones were directed towards the people of Egypt as now they will be towards the people of the world.

Although the first plague is poured out on the *land* it is *people* who are affected, specifically those people who have *the mark of the beast and have worshipped his image* (16:2). These belong to and acknowledge the leadership of one who rejects the rightful rule of God and his Messiah. They are part of an alternative and rebellious civilization who are living in God's world.

The second and third plagues are poured out on *sea* and *rivers/springs of water* which turn to *blood* (16:3–4). Everything in the sea died as a result. When the citizens of the beast come to drink from the water in the rivers and springs they find only "blood". Since they have shed the blood of saints and prophets these who belong to the community of the persecuting beast must drink "blood" in the rivers and springs. God's *judgments ... are true and just* (16:5–7).

127

The fourth plague is directed to the sun, in consequence of which *the sun was given power to scorch people with fire so that they were seared by the intense heat* (16:8–9).

The fifth plague, *darkness*, is poured out on *the throne of the beast and his kingdom*, that is, on all government and rule which is against God and which substitutes itself for God (16:10). Scorching heat is followed by darkness and presumably by coldness. As with the fourth plague the people cursed God and refused to repent or glorify him (16:11). But it is not yet time for the nations to come and worship God (cf 15:4).

The sixth plague is poured onto the *great river Euphrates*, which *dries up* and provides an easy access *for the kings of the East* (16:12). Rome's dreaded foes the Parthians came from Mesopotamia. Their mounted troops were prodigious horsemen capable of firing bow and arrow at full gallop. The Euphrates, unlike the Rhine and Danube, Rome's frontier to the north, provided no natural barrier to the East. It is noteworthy that the sixth trumpet which would destroy a third of mankind summoned myriads of cavalry from the Euphrates region (9:14). John is sensitive to the great dread people at that time had for these hordes from the east. Moreover, it was widely believed that the Emperor Nero would return from the dead and come from the East at the head of great armies to recapture Rome. As the first and greatest persecutor of Christians this was a fearsome prospect for Christians.

(3)   The interlude: the evil spirits and Armageddon (16:13–16)

Issuing from the mouths of the evil triad, *the dragon, the beast and the false prophet* (= the beast from the earth), were *frog*-like *evil spirits* which perform *miraculous signs*

(Greek: *semeia*). Whatever they are, and John doesn't elaborate, these have the appearance of true miracles as from God. They serve to influence and persuade *the kings of the whole world* (ie. not just from the East) to gather for battle, apparently in the belief that each is invincible. These demonic spirits *gathered the kings for battle . . . on the great day of God the Almighty . . . at the place that in Hebrew is called Armageddon* (16:14,16). This Armageddon takes its name from *Har* (Hebrew for mountain) of *Megiddo*, a fortified hill on the edge of and overlooking the Valley of Jezreel, scene of many a great battle in antiquity, located as it was on the main north-south, east-west routes through Palestine. This sixth plague is the horrendous, demon-inspired battle in which mankind will be destroyed by the kings of the whole world. How striking it is that the Dragon destroys his own, warranting the name given him earlier, *Apollyon/Abaddon* the "destroyer" (9:11).

John quickly reassures his Christian readers with words of Jesus (taken from Matthew 24:43, cf I Thessalonians 5:2; 2 Peter 3:10), *Behold I come like a thief!* (see 3:3). *Blessed is he who stays awake and keeps his clothes with him, so that he may not go naked and be shamefully exposed* (16:15). In calling his readers to watchfulness, as Jesus did, John is encouraging them that Jesus will come thief-like, unheralded, and that they have nothing to fear from Armageddon.

(4)   The seventh plague: the destruction of the air (16:17–21)

As the seventh angel pours out his bowl, a loud voice is heard from the throne, surely that of God crying out *"It is done"* (16:17). We are immediately reminded of the dying words of the Lord Jesus who in regard to the work of salvation which he had come to do cried out *"It is finished"* (John 19:30). In their original Greek form only one word is used in both cases. Each word, moreover, is in the perfect tense signifying a completed action with ongoing consequences. Because it is God who speaks, whether of salvation or of judgment, the word spoken comes to pass in history. God now says "Done" and the lightning, thunder, earthquake which follow splits great Babylon into three parts and destroys the cities of the nations.

More will be said of the destruction of Babylon in the following chapters. All that is said here, ominously, is *God remembered Babylon* (16:19). The recognisable frame of the creation of God disappears at his command, just as it had appeared originally at his word of command. *Every island fled ... and great mountains could not be found* (16:20). Great hailstones bombard people who still did not repent but *curse God on account of the plague of hail* (16:21). Even when it is "apocalypse now", when human and natural disasters engulf us, still we do not turn to our creator in acknowledgement. Mankind needs to hear the prophetic word, the eternal gospel. And we need to speak it, not least at times of catastrophe and disaster.

Of all the sequences in the Revelation there is none so apparently "prophetic" of the epoch in which we live. So much of this chapter strikes a chord with us today. The pollution of earth, rivers, sea and sky have reached near-apocalyptic dimensions, as the rise of the conservation movement bears witness. Mankind is faced with a diminishing ozone protection with attendant cancer perils from radiation. The so-called "greenhouse" effect brought about in part by the overconsumption of fossil fuel could soon bring massive flooding to huge and arable tracts of the low countries of the world, accompanied by large-scale displacement of peoples and drastic undersupply of food. And there is the ever-present threat of intercontinental as well as outer-space nuclear holocaust, the reality of which is testified to by world-wide street marches and demonstrations.

It is not surprising that the words "Armageddon" and "apocalyptic" are now part of the vocabulary of this generation. By all means let Christians march in the streets, demonstrate and protest. But above all let them not be people of despair, as many others around them are. Let them remember his words "Behold I come like a thief".

Thus the destruction of the "old heavens and earth" are now completed, clearing the way for the new creation of God. The message in all of this is that there is no future for us here in the old order, in the city of mankind, Babylon. The theology of Rome, which said an "eternal city" could be built, is wrong. It wasn't eternal, any more than the civilizations which preceded and which have come after, are eternal. They rise, then fall; they come, then go. Secular humanists, Marxist and others who believe a Utopia on earth is possible are also wrong, according to the Revelation. And they are wrong for the very simple reason that earthly rulers are corrupted by power and deify the power by which they are corrupted. Above all they will not acknowledge that the Lion of the tribe of Judah has conquered. Nor that the kingdom of the world has become the kingdom of our Lord and of his Christ, and that he, the Lord, will reign forever.

The eternal gospel of God's eternal kingdom is unpalatable to the kingdoms of humanity and for this reason evokes such ferocity and hostility. Politicians, kings and idealists cannot bear to hear that "fallen, fallen is Babylon the great", that there will be no paradise on earth, not now and not ever, however hard people work for it. They cannot accept that neither mankind nor society is perfectible in the old order. Yet this negative side of the gospel is as much a part of the gospel as that which declares that Jesus has saved and that he is Lord.

QUESTIONS ON REVELATION CHAPTERS 15–16:

1. How is the sequence of the bowls (16:2–21) different from the sequence of trumpets (8:6–9:21)?

2. Discuss the reasons for the difference between the response to God's final judgment (15:4) and the response to these plagues.

3. How are Christians urged to live in the face of such difficult circumstances (16:15)?

4. What is there in common between Jesus' "It is finished" (John 19:30) and "It is done" (16:17)? How does Revelation's author establish that there weren't two events, but one?

5. Discuss the message of this chapter in the light of our increasing environmental anxiety. How should we best arrive at a balanced view of God's final intervention in the created order *along with* the possibility of our own mismanaging of the earth and its resources?

6. How does the Bible see the relationship between the "cities of the nations" and "Babylon" (16:19)?

17

The end of evil 17-20

The destruction of the cosmos of God and of its
pinnacle, mankind, were the subject of the previous
section of the Revelation, chapters 15-16. Before the
new heavens and new earth as described in chapters
21-22 can become a reality, however, the sources of
evil must be eradicated.

Marxists believe that greed is the great evil which must
be removed before the new age can arrive. Secular humanists see the abolition of ignorance and poverty as
prerequisites to the emergence of the great society.
Christians agree that greed is a great evil and that the
education and health of our fellow-humans are among
the highest priorities for any community. Historically,
Christians have pioneered the provision of these minis-
tries; only in recent times have governments taken re-
sponsibility for hospitals and schools. Nonetheless, based
on Revelation and other New Testament teachings,
Christians regard evil as deeply entrenched within the
human personality, as in fact demonic and originating
ultimately from the great "deceiver of the nations".
Christians do not believe in the easy elimination of evil

nor in the perfectibility of society by human means.

The new age, therefore, will not arise from human endeavour; it will come neither by revolution nor by evolution, neither by the sword nor by quiet process. All that can come from below, from humanity, will be "more of the same". The technology will become more advanced and new "buzz words" about the coming of a new age will be used, but the principle of evil in one form or another will still be present. It has not yet been expunged.

Chapters 17–20 are important, therefore, because they depict, in the apocalyptist's words, the removal of supernatural evil in the defeat of the three evil personae who have warred against God and his people: the dragon, the beast, the false prophet (= the beast from the earth). These evil beings believe that they are about to engage with God and his armies in the last great battle which they, apparently, have every hope of winning. They are blind to the fact that the battle has already been fought and lost. God's final disposal of them, as it turns out in each case, proves to be an anti-climax, a non-event.

(1)   The fall of Babylon (17:1–19:8)

(a)   The woman and the beast (17)

The first supra-evil power to be overthrown is one whom John describes as *the great prostitute* (17:1) whom he identifies as the *great city that rules over the kings of the earth* (17:18), a clear reference to Rome and her dominance over her large empire. The *many waters* on which she sits is identified as the *peoples, multitudes, nations and languages* ruled by Roman power (17:15). Her clothing of *purple* and *scarlet* and adornment of *gold, precious stones* and *pearls* symbolize her imperial and regal status (17:3).

She holds a *golden cup* filled, on one hand with *her adulteries* with the *kings of the earth* (17:2,4–5), and on the other, with *the blood of the saints*, with which she is *drunk* (17:6). In her great wealth and power, Rome seduces the rulers of the world to trade with her, regardless of the best interests of the indigenous citizens. Her godless standards spread throughout the world. Intolerant of any nonconformity, she pursues and kills any group (like the Christians) who will not give absolute allegiance to her. The nations of the world are now attacking God's people, in imitation of Rome (18:23). Doubtless John has in mind the multitude of believers slaughtered in Rome by the Emperor Nero in AD 64. But this assault is being repeated elsewhere within the empire, for example proconsular Asia (18:23–24).

She is seated on the *beast*, whom we have already encountered (13:1), and who is to be identified as the Roman emperor. Like the woman, he too, is *scarlet* in colour, signifying imperial status. The *blasphemous names* (17:3) remind us of the idolatrous and pretentious character of the imperial cult to which John's original readers were subject.

As previously described the beast (= Emperor) has *seven heads* and *ten horns* (13:1). The latter are here identified with *ten kings who have not yet received a kingdom but who for one hour receive authority as kings along with the beast* (17:12). These are probably the governors who, in senatorial provinces like proconsular Asia, served for only one year (Dio Cassius, *Roman History*, xii–xv). Their authority, like that of the beast, derives from the Dragon (13:2) and their *one purpose* is to *give power and authority to the beast.* As instruments of the beast, these governors *make war against the Lamb* (17:13–14 cf 13:7).

John gives multiple meanings to the *seven heads*. On one hand these are the *seven hills* (17:9) on which Rome is located. These seven heads are also *seven kings*, about which much has been written by scholars. These are in veiled reference to the emperors who had to that point ruled the Roman world. The view taken here is that:

the *five* [who] *have fallen* are	Augustus, Tiberius, Gaius, Claudius and Nero
the *one* [who] *is* is	Vespasian (AD 69–79)
the *other* [who] is not yet come and who *must remain a little while* is	Titus (Emperor AD 79–81)
the beast who once was and now is not, is an eighth king ...	Domitian (AD 81–96)
belongs to the seven and is going to destruction	as Nero "re-incarnate"

Nero loomed large for Christians in the last quarter of the first century. He was their first persecutor. It was widely believed that he was to return from the dead at the head of mighty armies and resume his place as emperor, something that would strike terror into the hearts of Christians. John does not hold this view. The only way Nero is thought of as returning is in the person of Domitian the new persecutor, who, however is heading for destruction.

John portrays Nero/Domitian as a kind of parody of God's true ruler, the Lion of the tribe of Judah. Just as Jesus **was** (incarnation), and **is not** (ascension) but **will come again** (parousia), so too, in John's presentation, Nero *once was, now is not* and yet *will come*. But unlike

Jesus who will come from heaven and take up his ever-lasting rule over all things, this beast, this pretentious ruler, will come up *out of the Abyss* and *go to his destruction* (17:8,11). John defers for the moment his description of the destruction of the beast.

(b)   The fall of Babylon (18)

How ironical it is that the woman is overthrown not by her enemies but by those closest to her, by *the beast* himself and the *ten horns* who *hate the prostitute . . . and bring her to ruin* (17:15–16). The great city will fall not because of an invader but because of her own ruler. This is a surprising comment given the preoccupation most civilizations have had with external threats to their security. While such fears have often been well-founded, it is significant that few civilizations have seen their destruction coming from within.

In a long and lyrical passage John now turns to describe the fall of this city, which he designates as *Babylon the Great*. The greatness of her immense wealth (18:11–13) is matched only by her corrupting of those who trade with her (18:3,9), on one hand, and by her crimes against the saints on the other (18:20,24). Despite her awesome power and her self-glorification, she is in reality a seductress and her evils have now been disseminated universally.

Accordingly Babylon will come under the judgment of God. A voice from heaven says *her sins are piled up to heaven and God has remembered her crimes* (18:5) and *mighty is the God who judges her* (18:8).

John prophesies at some length about her downfall. *Fallen! Fallen! is Babylon the Great . . . Woe! Woe! O great city, O Babylon, city of power . . .* (18:2,9,19). Despite her glory, greatness and power (18:18), she shall fall quickly, *in one day, in one hour* (18:8,9,17,19). She is no "eternal city" as she supposed; in a moment God will cast her down, never to recover (18:22). Never again will be heard there the sound of *music*, or of *bridegroom and bride*, never again will be found any *workman of any trade*, never again will be seen the *light of lamp* (18:21–23). She shall become desolate and uninhabited, except by *demons, evil spirits and every unclean and detestable bird* (18:2).

Babylon the tawdry whore will be no more; in her place God will bring the new Jerusalem, the pure and beautiful bride of the Lamb (21:2). Thus those who belong to the bride of the Lamb, persecuted as she now is (12:17), are exhorted to *come out* (18:4) of Babylon the prostitute and to resist her seductive ways. God's people can have no part in her worship of the beast nor in the judgment of God which will soon ensue.

John's prophecy of the fall of imperial Rome is remarkable. At the time he wrote the Revelation, during the nineties, Rome was at the height of her powers. There was no serious threat to her frontiers nor any sign of major uprising from her own subject peoples. Pirates had been cleared from the seas and brigands from the countryside. Elegant cities dotted the shores of the Mediterranean and were to be found in many inland regions as well. Soon the tyrant Domitian would fall and the empire would enter the golden years of the "five good emperors", Nerva, Trajan, Hadrian, Antoninus Pius and Marcus Aurelius, spanning AD 96–180. Those who read the Revelation during those years must have found John's prophecy of the fall of "Babylon" very difficult to believe.

John's reference to Babylon, however, arises from the many references to that city/civilization in the Old Testament. She is "Babel", the city built by the descendants of those driven from the garden of God. These fugitives

138

from the divine judgment build a metropolis to make for **themselves** a name and to resist being scattered further by the God to whom they will not return in humility and repentance (Genesis 11:1–4). In God's judgment on her, Babel will never be completed and her citizens will not speak the same language, will not understand one another (11.5–9). This city built for the name of mankind will lack permanency; it will be marked by alienation and disunity.

Moreover, with the passage of time the people of Jerusalem, the city of God, will be found as captives within pagan and powerful Babylon. They will weep in Babylon as they remember distant Jerusalem and as they submit to the taunts of their tormenters (Psalm 137).

In Isaiah Babylon is portrayed as a proud, Satan-like being who aspires to be equal with God saying "I will make myself like the Most High" (Isaiah 14:14). This brutal city "subdued nations with relentless aggression" (Isaiah 14:6) and inflicted great suffering on the people of God. God will bring down this evil civilization and leave it desolate (Isaiah 14:22–23). It is clear that John has prophesied the fall of Rome through the reading of Isaiah 14:3–23.

John has also seen Rome as "Babylon" through the reading of Isaiah 47. God had allowed his people to go into captivity into Babylon. Babylon, however, "showed them no mercy" and "even on the aged . . . laid a heavy yoke" (47:6,7). Babylon proudly usurped the place of God by taking his name, saying "**I am**; there is none else beside me" (47:8 cf Exodus 3:14). In her own eyes she is eternal and divine. "No one sees me", she said, denying any deity beside herself (47:10). "I will never be a widow nor suffer the loss of children", she said, claiming immunity from judgment and catastrophe (47:8). But God said to Babylon "Both of these will overtake you in a moment, on a single day" (47:9).

For John, then, Rome was "Babylon", a civilization in revolt against God and his kingdom, a community which warred against God and the people who bear faithful witness that he alone is God. Thus John, after careful reflection on passages like Isaiah 14 and 47 declares that "Fallen! Fallen! Is Babylon the great". It must not be thought, however, that God judges "Babylon" simply because it is a city or a civilization per se, or that God condemns the human culture that flourished in ancient Babylon or, for that matter, imperial Rome. God's judgment falls on that society, ancient or modern, which usurps the place of God and which oppresses the people who worship the creator and who decline to worship as god either the state or its ruler.

(c)   Hallelujah! (19:1–8)

Once again we encounter the two-beat rhythm of evangelic declaration and worshipful response. First, the great multitudes of heaven shout the gospel message that *Salvation and glory and power belong to our God, for true and just are his judgments. He has condemned the great prostitute ... Praise our God* (19:1,2,). Unpalatable as it is, we need to accept that the second advent will be characterised by the judgment of God and that this will be directed at societies and rulers which usurp the place of God and not just at men and women as individuals. As we have commented more than once, this too is part of the gospel though we seldom recognise it as such.

In reply a great multitude shout *Hallelujah! For our Lord God Almighty reigns. Let us rejoice and be glad and give him glory!* (19:6–7). True worship is the thankful reply of the people to the gospel of God. Those who blaspheme the name of God and war against his faithful

140

people will be overthrown; they will not continue forever.

Because the prostitute is fallen the time of the bride of the Lamb has now come. Note once again the parallelism between the false ruler and the true, between the corrupt city and the New Jerusalem, and between the evil woman and the pure bride of Christ. The victory of God for which his people praise him is not just that the prostitute is overthrown, but that *the wedding of the Lamb has come and his bride has made herself ready* (19:7–8). Perhaps it is those who have been tested in the fires of persecution who most long for their Lord's return.

(d)   The spirit of prophecy (19:9–10)

At the time it may easily have seemed that the persecu- tors were well off and the believers accursed. The angel told John that those *invited to the wedding supper of the Lamb* were the truly *blessed* ones. So important was this that John was directed to *write* it down for the sake of his readers, adding *these are the true words of God*. Believers must allow God's words of promise to them to outweigh their fears.

John was so struck by the words of the angel that he fell down in worship, only to be rebuked. An angel is a mere fellow-servant. Christians are not likely to err as pagans do by worshipping idols and demons. But they may, perhaps, be inclined to worship angels. (Colossians 2:18 and Hebrews 1:6–7; 2:5 suggest that Jewish Christians may have been tempted in that direction.) The angel's admonition *Worship God* (19:10) is a warning not to make the same mistake.

The *testimony of Jesus* could be summed up in the words "worship God". This is, in effect, the message of the Revelation. But that testimony of Jesus is also *the spirit*, or the essence, of prophecy (19:10). The message of John the prophet, like that of Jesus whom he served, is one and the same: "worship God".

(2)   The capture of the beast and the false prophet (19:11–21)

The scene is set for a great, last battle. Pitted against each other are the *armies of heaven* following the *king of kings and lord of lords* (19:14,16) versus the armies of the *beast and the kings of the earth* (19:19).

John sees heaven standing open and there before him is Jesus, resembling in appearance John's initial vision of him on Patmos (19:11–16; cf 1:12–18). He is a powerful and victorious figure, as may be seen by his *eyes* which are *like blazing fire*, the *many crowns* on his head and the *white horse* he rides (white signifying triumph). In his mouth is a *sharp sword* (cf 1:16; 2:12) to *strike down the nations* whom he will *rule with an iron sceptre* (Psalm 2:9 cf 12:5). John saw that with *justice he judges and makes war* (19:11) and that he *treads the winepress of the fury of the wrath of God Almighty* (19:15). This, then, is the fearsome image of Jesus that John saw in the opened heavens: victor, ruler, judge and executioner.

But this is only one half of the picture. Just as the Lion of the tribe of Judah turned out to be a Lamb with a death wound, so the victorious horseman is seen to be triumphant not through military victory, but through faithfulness in death. His *robe* is *dipped in blood* (19:13) and he is called *Faithful and True* (19:11). His name is the *Word of God* (19:13) which is the only sword to be found in the mouth of Jesus. He is followed by the armies of heaven riding on white horses, signifying their victory. His people share his victory throughout and at the end of history (cf 2:27). But theirs is a victory of righteousness since the *fine linen* they wear stands for the *righteous acts of the saints* (19:8). In a dazzling shift of imagery John depicts the faithful people of God now as a *bride* in fine linen (19:7–8), now as the *armies* of heaven in fine linen (19:14).

By his use of images John is portraying Jesus in his second coming as a conqueror, a pierced (cf 1:7), blood-stained, faithful conqueror, whose followers are victorious in virtue of their righteousness. In the period before he returns in triumph, which is the period in which we live, he rules the nations with the sword of his mouth, which is the word of God/the testimony of Jesus, that his followers speak. He exercises his rule not by military might or by a politically triumphalist church, but by the gospel which his righteous people speak. Even in the final judgment it will be by the sword in Jesus' mouth, namely the word of God, that he executes judgment (19:21). That is the only sword to be wielded by Jesus.

The *beast* and the *kings of the earth* hopefully assemble their armies to make *war against the rider of the white horse and his army* (19:19). But it is a vain, futile effort. The battle is past and it is lost. Even before the beast's final rallying cry the angel summons the *birds* to gather for the *great supper of God* (19:17) where they will eat the *flesh of kings, generals and mighty men* (19:18).

There is no battle. In a complete anticlimax and with a total absence of drama the *beast* and *false prophet*, representing the emperor and cultic high priest respectively, are simply *captured* and consigned to the *fiery lake* (19:20). The human supporters of beast and false prophet are killed and their flesh eaten by the birds.

Why does it end so tamely for the beast and the false prophet? As we frequently observed, it is because the Lion of the tribe of Judah **has** conquered as the Lamb that was slain but lives (5:5–6). In the death and resurrection of Jesus, God has taken his great power and

143

begun to reign (11:16). The kingdom of the world then became the kingdom of our Lord and of his Christ (11:16). When the rider on the white horse finally comes there is no battle to be fought but only a word to be spoken. And evil will be no more.

(3)   The end of the dragon (20:1–10)

(a)   The final overthrow of the dragon (20:7–10)

After being bound for *one thousand years* Satan is *released* from *his prison* and will for *a short period* again *deceive the nations* (20:7,3). We defer for a moment discussing the meaning of the prison and the one thousand years. The nations deceived by Satan are specified, in particular, as *Gog* and *Magog*. In Ezekiel 38:2, the only Old Testament passage where both names occur, Gog is an evil prince from the land of Magog. In later Judaism the names Gog and Magog symbolize evil and it is in that sense they appear to be used by John. Satan gathers Gog and Magog for battle. The nations led by Gog and Magog *surround the camp* (of the armies) *of God's people*, which is explained as *the city of God* (20:9). It seems that the now-liberated dragon, in his final deception of the nations, will make a final assault on the people of God. This suggests there will be a period of severe persecution on earth before Satan is finally overthrown. This persecution will be only for a short time.

Once again the forces of evil attempt to precipitate a great and final battle which apparently they expect to win (cf 16:14,16; 19:19). Are these three separate attempts to engage with God in a last battle? In keeping with the author's style in which he repeats ideas and concepts in the different sequences, we should see these not as three events but as one event. The final overthrow of the dragon should be seen as occurring at the same time as the other members of the evil triad, the beast and the false prophet. Each evil personage is consigned to the lake of fire.

In a completely anticlimactic way, *fire came down from heaven and devoured* the armies of the nations, and the dragon was cast into the lake of burning sulphur, just as the beast and the false prophet had been (20:10). Despite the expectations of the dragon he, like the beast and the false prophet, is dispatched quickly, without ceremony or struggle. To use T.S. Eliot's famous phrase, these things end not with a bang, but with a whimper. Thus God removes the sources of evil from any further influence, in preparation for his gift of a new heavens and a new earth.

(b)   The one thousand years (20:1-6)

Few questions of interpretation are so divisive among Christians as those applied to this passage. From the first decades after the writing of the Revelation down to our own day there have been many who have interpreted the thousand years in a literal manner. According to this view Christ returns to earth to cast the beast and the false prophet into the fiery lake and to consign the dragon to a prison for one thousand years. At the end of a millennium of peace on earth Satan is released for a brief and chaotic period before Jesus finally returns to conclude history.

Against this widely held view it should be noted that Revelation 20:1-6 is the only part of the Bible to mention the one thousand years. This is the basis of the doctrine known in early times as Chiliasm and referred to today as pre-millennialism (or dispensationalism). Further, it is argued that this numeral, like other numerals within the Revelation, is symbolic (144,000, for example). Is it not precarious to build so important a doctrine on so brief and so figurative a passage?

145

As it happens the one thousand years is defined as beginning with the *first resurrection* (20:5) and ending at the *second death* (20:6). The first resurrection is Christ's historic resurrection, when those who will lose their lives in faithful witness will (spiritually speaking) be raised with him (20:4,6). The second death is when the dragon is sent into the fiery lake, presumably at the time of Christ's second coming. The one thousand years is that span of time, however long it proves to be, separating Christ's resurrection from his return.

What then does it mean for the dragon to be *bound* (20:2) in *prison* (20:7) for the one thousand years? The answer to this question is closely related to the fact that the faithful martyrs came to life in the first resurrection and *reign with Christ* for *one thousand years* (20:4–5). Christ enters his reign by virtue of his sacrificial death, by which the dragon is defeated (cf 12:11). His reign is shared by his people who, in their uncompromised faithfulness to him, have laid down their lives. According to chapter 12 "the brothers . . . overcame him [the dragon] by the blood of the Lamb and by the word of their testimony because they loved not their lives unto death" (verse 11).

In other words, Satan is "bound" or restricted in his activities throughout the period between Christ's resurrection and his return, by the faithfulness to the death of Christian believers. Positively, they have been prepared to die because of *their testimony for Jesus and because of the word of God*. Negatively, *they had not worshipped the beast or his image nor received his mark on their foreheads or their hands* (20:4).

How are we to think of these believers who have remained faithful to Jesus throughout their lives? According to John they *came to life* in *the first resurrection* and *reign with Christ* throughout the *thousand years, seated . . . on*

146

thrones and are *given authority to judge* (20:4); through-out the thousand years *they will be priests of God and of Christ* (20:6). Those who have borne costly witness in life and word to Jesus will not be defeated by either the first death (biological) nor the second death (the fiery lake). All others must await the end of the thousand years before their resurrection and the outcome of the judg-ment of God. But the faithful ones who have shared in Jesus' death by their witness to it will share in his victory, his thousand year reign, his priesthood and his judgment. Notice that John recognises only one kind of Christian: those who are faithful to death! John does not explain the relationship between the redemptive death of the Lamb and the faithfulness of believers in the binding of Satan. Clearly Jesus' death has absolute power. He is the con-quering "Lion of Judah" as the "Lamb that was slain" (5:5–6). Nonetheless, his people share in and apply his victory, positively, as they speak the word of God in testimony for Jesus and, negatively, as they resist the great pressure put on them to worship the emperor and his statue. Though defeated and cast down by Christ at the first Easter, the dragon still deceives the nations and makes war on believers throughout the whole period before the second advent of Jesus. He is imprisoned, bound and restricted throughout that period, however, by the faithful ministry and confession of Christians.

The wane of Christianity in the West during the latter decades of the 20th century has witnessed the re-emergence of witchcraft, the occult and other satanic activities. Film–makers have become very interested in the Devil, demons, possession by evil spirits and the theme of exorcism. Recently, various Christian groups have given the Devil much greater attention than for many years.

While the fact and influence of Satan should not be ignored, Christians must not forget – as they are prone to do – that the Evil One has been defeated by Christ's death and resurrection and is bound and limited by the gospel and by courageous Christian witness. There is a tendency for Christians to take a minimal view of the historic victory of Christ, and to emphasise instead various techniques such as exorcism and prayer counselling. Let it be understood that it is not by techniques, but by the redemptive death of Jesus and the ongoing preaching of the cross, that the Devil is defeated and bound.

(4)   The second death (20:11–15)

Deceased believers are, as we have seen, not dead but alive, reigning with Christ throughout the "thousand years" between the resurrection and the return of Jesus. What then of the rest of humanity? John makes no comment, as Paul does (I Thessalonians 4.13–18) about those who are still alive at the coming of the Lord.

John reserves his comments for *the dead*, whom he says, *come to life* after the thousand years are *ended* (20:5). Thus *the sea, death and Hades* (= the place of the dead), *gave up the dead* that were in them (20.13). John now depicts the dead, *great and small, as standing before* God who is *seated on the great white throne*. It is a scene of awesome holiness. *Earth and sky fled from the presence* of him who is seated on the throne. But there is no escape for those who stand there before God.

The books are *now opened*, that is by God (as the divine passive implies) . . . books which *recorded* what the dead *had done* during their lives (20:12). Each person is now judged (by God, the divine passive again) *according to what they had done* (20:12,13). God the enthroned judge of all will pass judgment according to the deeds of the dead, who now stand raised to life before him.

148

What will be the outcome of this last, final judgment? Will they pass or fail? Examinees must patiently await the publication of the results and there is always some uncertainty. But there is no uncertainty about the results of this "examination". If one's name is not found in the book of life, that is, the list of those who belong to the Lamb, then one's future is in the lake of fire (20:15).

Clearly the deeds in life of each and every person will condemn them when the books are opened. Only those who during their lives have fled to the Lamb for mercy and who have faithfully lived and testified for him and whose names, therefore, are written in the Lamb's book of life (13:8; 17:8) are alive and reigning with him. All others will indeed be raised to life, but they will be subjected to the judgment of God and condemned to share the fate of those whom they have worshipped and served: the dragon, the beast and the false-prophet. This evil triad and their community of worshippers and servants are destined for the lake of fire.

The language here as elsewhere in the Revelation is symbolic and pictorial, but that in no way lessens the underlying reality. Nor should the logistics involved in gathering and judging so many provoke doubts about the truth of the judgment of God. (John Wesley thought the judgment would last one thousand years!). We must not reduce God by our own calculations. Rather, the fact of last judgment should provoke us to bring the gospel to every person so that they turn in repentance and faith to the redeemer-Lamb. Moreover, we who are believers should find in the great judgment an ongoing caution against spiritual laxity and laziness.

QUESTIONS ON REVELATION CHAPTERS 17–20:

1. What are the characteristics of Babylon (17:2–6), and how do they affect Christians?

2. Is Babylon destroyed by enemies or friends (17: 16–17)? What does this teach us about the nature of evil?

3. To what extent is Nero/Domitian portrayed as a parody of Jesus (17:8–11)?

4. Why does God judge Babylon? What light does this shed on the nature of corruption, and the way we might evaluate corporate or national success?

5. Is it a problem that Jesus seems so different in his second advent (19:11–16)? Why/why not?

6. Discuss the two-sided character of Jesus as described in 19:11–16.

7. What does Revelation describe as being the beginning and the end of the one thousand years (20:4–6)?

8. What does John mean by saying that Satan was "bound" (20:2–3)? Is he bound today?

18

New Jerusalem 21–22

(1)   New heaven and a new earth (21:1–4)

The disappearance of the existing framework of the universe has been anticipated on a number of occasions in the Revelation (6:12–14; 8:7–12; 16:2–9) so that John's statement that the first heaven and the *first earth had passed away* (literally "departed") *and there was no more any sea* comes as no surprise. Since the dragon, the [sea] beast and the false prophet = the [earth] beast are no more (19:20; 20:10), it is inappropriate that their habitat — heaven, earth and sea — should remain. Not only evil, but also the environment of evil, will be no more.

This teaching is in sharp contrast to world-views of Marxists and secular humanists who envisage a new age arising out of, and in continuity with, the existing order. John does not teach a new order in continuity with, but in **discontinuity** with, the present creation.

His prophecy is entirely in line with Isaiah who wrote:

I will create new heavens and a new earth
The former things will not be remembered,
nor will they come to mind (65:17, NIV)

Isaiah continued immediately . . .

But be glad and rejoice forever in what I will create,
for I will create Jerusalem to be a delight
and its people a joy.

What John then saw *coming down out of heaven from God*, in fulfilment of Isaiah's promise, was *the Holy City, the New Jerusalem*. It has come, not by peaceful evolution nor by violent revolution, but by God's gift from heaven.

This city is further described as *a bride beautifully dressed for her husband*. The woman desperately men-aced and pursued on earth by the dragon (12:4,6,13–17) is now the pristine bride of the Lamb, coming in serene beauty from heaven (cf 21:9; 19:7). She is the community of those faithful and enduring ones who, in their deaths, have been raised with Christ in the first resurrection and who have been reigning with him throughout the thou-sand years (20:4–6).

Here is an astonishing teaching. The New Heaven and New Earth is the New Jerusalem which is the Bride of Christ, both of which depict the gathered community of the redeemed ones. The new creation is the church, the church of the end-time.

Notice once more the contrastive parallelism used by John. On one hand there is the community of the beast, the people of the Roman Empire, who worship Caesar and his image, and who are pictorially referred to as a city ("Babylon the Great", 17:5) and as a woman ("the great prostitute", 17:1). This community has brought great misery to its opposite number, the community of Christian believers, who are also depicted as a city ("new Jerusalem") and as a woman ("the wife of the Lamb"). The community of the beast is now overtaken and re-placed by the community of the Lamb; New Jerusalem replaces Babylon, the Bride of the Lamb replaces the great prostitute.

First John saw; now he hears. A *loud voice* from the *throne*, which must mean that the speaker is God, said: *the dwelling* (tabernacle/tent) *of God is now with men and . . . he will live with them.* These words spring from two Old Testament passages: Leviticus 26:12–13 and Ezekiel 37:27–28. In the former, God promises to make his dwelling with the people when he rescues them from slavery in Egypt. In the latter, God identifies his dwelling among them in terms of his sanctuary or temple, which will be a sign to the nations that he is his people's God. The time has now come when God has finally rescued his people, when he is himself present with them as their temple. John may also be referring to the second advent of Jesus, when he would once more "tabernacle" (cf John 1:14) with his people as God with them, but now permanently, never again to be separated.

God, now present with his people, *will wipe away every tear from their eyes.* The bride of Christ whose blood has been drunk by the harlot, the city Jerusalem which has suffered so much exiled in Babylon, is now comforted by her God. Again John is deeply influenced by Isaiah, in the continuation of the passage quoted above:

I will rejoice over Jerusalem and take delight in my people; the sound of weeping and of crying will be heard in it no more (65:19, **NIV**).

Thus John writes *there will be no more death or mourning or crying or pain.* All that he has suffered on Patmos, and all that his fellow-Christians have endured in the cities of Roman Asia from the hands of the authorities, on account of their loyalty to Jesus as against Caesar, will come to an end. The passage speaks of the end of pain and death, but it should be noted that this refers, in the first instance, to the cessation of suffering which has been endured through persecution in loyalty to Christ.

(2)   The evangelic challenge (21:5–8)

The Enthroned One now utters three further statements to John. First, he declares the divine plan to the prophet: *I am making everything new*: there will be a new creation comprising God's people with whom he will dwell. Second, God assures John that *these words are **trustworthy** and **true*** (cf 3:14; 19:11, where these two words are a title of Jesus). He commands John to *write this down*; the promise of the new creation comes from God and is reliable. Third, he announces the fulfilment of the plan in what is in the original language one word, *it is done* (Greek: *gegonan* cf 16:17). The plan will certainly be fulfilled because of the identity of the speaker, who declares *I am* the alpha and the omega, the beginning and the end. The divine I AM overarches history, knowing its beginning from its end. He who speaks the promise brings it to fulfilment. Therefore he speaks with authority and truth and his words are to be believed.

God continues to speak, first to those who will belong to the Holy City and then to those who will not. To *the thirsty*, that is to those exhausted from the struggle to remain Christian against the great pressure of the beast and the false prophet, God offers the water of life which will flow freely in the City (22:1): *I will give to drink without cost from the spring of the water of life*. These words resemble two promises of Jesus as found in the Gospel of John ("If a man is thirsty . . . " in 7:37; "The water I will give him will become . . . a spring of water welling up to eternal life" in 4:13), and strengthen the belief that the author of the Revelation also wrote the fourth Gospel. Those *who overcome*, that is, who conquer the forces pitted against them which would make them abandon the faith, will *inherit* the New Jerusalem. Moreover, God will be their God and they will be God's children.

By contrast, however, and in parallel with the redeemed community who are the new Jerusalem, the Bride of the Lamb, there will be those destined for the *fiery lake*, what John calls the *second death*. These may be subdivided into lapsed Christians (the *cowardly*, the *unbelieving* = faithless, the *vile* = polluted) and those who have only ever belonged to the community of the beast and the false prophet (*the murderers, the sexually immoral, those who practise magic arts, the idolators and all liars*). Clearly John is exhorting and encouraging his readers to continue as Christians and not to give up the struggle. The alternative community of the faithless face a grim future.

(3)   The splendour and immensity of the holy city (21:9–21)

John is addressed once more by an angel with a bowl full of the seven last plagues. Possibly it is the same angel who had summoned John earlier: "Come I will show you the punishment of the great prostitute" (17:1). Now, however, to balance the symmetry in the contrastive parallelism, the angel says: *"Come I will show you the bride, the wife of the Lamb"*. As we have noted already, this woman is the church on earth who had been persecuted and tear-stained but who is now secure, protected and restored by God, ready for her marriage with her husband, the redeemer-Lamb.

What the angel showed [John], however, was not a woman, but the *Holy City, Jerusalem, coming down out of heaven from God*. Those who read need to keep alert to John's rapidly changing imagery. At the beginning of the chapter the Holy City is mentioned before the beautifully dressed bride. Here the order is reversed. Both images represent the gathered and redeemed people of God.

Three characteristics of the city are now established in pictorial terms. It is, first, a city which *shines with the glory of God*. In contrast to the haunted, doomed, smouldering Babylon (18:9) the angel showed John a city brilliant in light and colour *like that of a very precious jewel, like jasper, clear as crystal* (21:12). *The foundations of the city walls were decorated with every kind of precious stone* (21:19) and *the walls* as well as the foundations were made of *jasper* (21:18) and the *twelve gates were made of pearl* (21:21). The *city* and its *streets* were made of *gold, as transparent as glass* (21:18,21).

If the first creation of God is beautiful, as it truly is, then these images of the City of God teach us that the new creation is to be infinitely more glorious. As with the first creation the source of the beauty is not mankind but God. Ugliness and destruction in the world are due almost entirely to humanity; goodness and beauty in the old and the new creations are due to God. Men and women are indeed able to create beauty but when they do so it is in imitation of the beauty of God's creation. When people attempt to be creative apart from God, their efforts are frequently debased and corrupt. Our hope for a future which is bright with glory does not lie with Caesar or his modern political counterparts, or with architects, town-planners or the artistically creative, but with God.

The second characteristic of the city is its size. The angel who showed John the city also measured its length, width and height. It was, in fact, a perfect cube, but of enormous proportions. What John saw descending from God was vast, 2250 kilometres (= 12,000 stadia) long, wide and high — from Adelaide to Brisbane or almost London to Athens cubed! In John's time that distance in every direction was probably as big as the known world, located as it was around the shores of the Mediterranean. John is saying that the city, the new creation, was huge, co-extensive with the present creation.

Third, the city is founded on God's redemptive acts. The number twelve is important here. The *twelve gates* bore the names of the *twelve tribes of Israel* (21:12). The *twelve foundations* of the city *wall* had on them the names of *the twelve apostles* of the Lamb (21:13). Only those obedient to God as members of Israel in the old covenant, on one hand, and to the message of the apostles of the Lamb under the new covenant on the other, will be part of the city of God.

The city of God is now present. The created world and history have finally been overtaken by God's purposes. The end of the Bible's story is at hand. Babel/Babylon, the city of mankind in rebellion against God, the civilization which had always been harsh to the people of God domiciled within her, the community which despite its best efforts to achieve unity and solidarity was always one of internal hostility and alienation, is no more. The dwelling of God is with men and women, he will live with them (21:3).

(4)   Worship in the holy city (21:22–22:5)

And his servants shall worship (Greek: *latreuein*) *him* (22:3 RSV). As the Revelation began with worship ("John . . . in the Spirit . . . on the Lord's Day" 1:9,10), so it concludes. John's readers are confronted with the challenge of whom they shall worship: the Beast and its image or the Enthroned One and the Lamb? At the time John wrote, the Emperor Domitian sought to be called "Lord and God" and had a large statue of himself erected in a specially constructed temple in Ephesus, the leading city of the province. Recent times had seen a remarkable

157

proliferation of the imperial cult in Roman Asia. John says repeatedly 'do not worship the beast' (14:9,11; 16:2; 19:20; 20:4); *worship God* (15:4; 19:4,10; 22:8). It is for this reason John so frequently portrays the redeemed and the angelic hosts proclaiming and acclaiming worthiness of the Lord God Almighty and the Lamb that was slain. Worship, however, must not be thought of only in terms of singing the praises of God, important as that might be. Rather, worship is the settled attitude of heart and mind towards the true source of power, truth and reality in life. John says, repeatedly, worship God.

At that time Satan deceived the hearts of people to believe that Caesar and the Roman State were worthy to receive reverence and honour. At this present time political leaders in both the communist bloc and the democratic societies tend to portray themselves as "saviours" of the people and that a "new age" will begin when they are elected or appointed. The electronic media beckon us to use consumer durables and other goods so as to fulfil our deepest needs, in what is almost a religious sense. God's people need to identify the pseudo-salvations and pseudo-saviours in every generation and to determine to give their worship only to God and the Lamb. This worship is for the whole of life in every situation. Certainly the verbal worship of God in the church meeting is a vital focal point of that greater worship, though it is not by any means the totality of worship.

There are two notable absences from this city. John states that he did not see a temple in the city of God. Here the Revelation is curiously bewildering for its readers. Earlier in the book there are many references to the temple. Christ promised the Philadelphians who overcame the opposing forces: "I will make a pillar in the temple of my God" (3:12). Those who came out of the great tribulation "serve [God] day and night in his temple" (7:15). When God finally takes his great power and begins to reign, "God's temple in heaven [is] opened" (11:19). How is it, then, that 21:22 states that there is no temple when there are numerous earlier statements which affirm the existence of the temple of God?

The answer is that, as John declares, the *Lord God Almighty and the Lamb are* [the city's] *temple.* Under the new covenant the people approach God directly, without human priestly mediation and without a sacred shrine. It will be remembered that Jesus taught that if the temple were to be destroyed, another temple would be raised after three days. According to John this temple was Jesus' body (John 2:19–21). The body of the risen Lord would henceforth be the place to meet God, the place where God now dwelt. From the first Easter, therefore, there was no longer a place for the temple or temple worship, in the unfolding purposes of God (see John 4:23–24).

In the city, God and the Lamb will be worshipped directly and immediately, without a temple. The worship there of God and the Lamb are to be vital activities.

Also absent from the city are the celestial lights of sun and moon. The city has no need of the illumination given by these; *the glory of God gives it light, and the Lamb is its lamp* (21:23). Light was God's gift to the old creation to enable people to see, springing into being as the first command of the Lord, and being pronounced "good" by God (Genesis 1:3–4). The people needed spiritual and moral light, as well as physical light. The psalmist wrote: "In your light we see light" (Psalm 36:9). In the new creation, the City of God, the people will still be dependent on light which will be provided by God and the Lamb.

The city is, of course, people. It is a human environment. But which people? John saw the nations (= the Gentiles) brought into the city, a reminder of the ancient promise by God to Abraham that "through his offspring all nations on earth will be blessed" (Genesis 22:18; Galatians 3:8). Through Abraham's "offspring", Jesus Christ, God reached out to all the nations of the world. The small and struggling churches of Roman Asia are not to limit their view of the composition of the city by their own straightened circumstances. *The nations will walk by its light, and the kings of the earth will bring their splendour into it* (21:24). Because of the glory of God permanently irradiating the city, night will never fall; there will be no darkness. *On no day will the gates of the city ever be shut* (21:25), as they customarily are at nightfall in ancient cities. The light of God and of the Lamb will perfectly shine, as gates of the city remain open and the peoples of the world and their rulers stream in.

But not all may enter. Those destined for the "fiery lake", as referred to earlier (21:8), will not be permitted access. The *impure* and those *who [do] what is shameful or deceitful* (21:27) are denied admission. These derive their impurity and shame by their participation in the sins of the alternative, evil community which is destined for the "fiery lake": murder, sexual immorality, magic, idolatry and lies (21:8). The members of that other "city" will not enter the City of God but only those *whose names are written in the Lamb's book of life.* The contrastive parallelism underlying the Revelation surfaces once again. The "fiery lake" is the destination of the Beast, the false prophet and their loyal community whereas people loyal to the Lamb will be present with the Lord God Almighty and the Lamb in the City of God. One community worships the Beast and its image whereas the other community worships the Lord God Almighty and the Lamb.

The theme of worship is implicit in the picture of *the river of the water of life, flowing from the throne of God and of the Lamb, through the middle of the street of the city* (22:1–2). Descriptions of a river flowing out of the temple and out of Jerusalem appear in the writings of the prophets (Ezekiel 47:1–12; Zechariah 14:8). These prophecies teach, on one hand, that God's kingship is over all his creation and, on the other, that the worship of God is to be universal. God and the Lamb from whose throne the river flows, as we have just been told (21:22), are the temple in the City of God. The twin themes of kingship and worship are also to be found here.

The river reminds us of the paradise of God in the garden of Eden, as found in Genesis 2, which has in turn provided inspiration for the prophets' vision of the future. *The tree of life*, also found in Genesis 2, is seen growing either side of the river which flows through the middle of the *great*, main *street* of the city. The tree appears to be more like a noble vine of infinite length which bears *twelve kinds of fruit* for *each month* of the year, a picture of the everlasting, never-ending character of the "life" now available for the people of the city. The *leaves* from that tree are *for the healing of the nations*. The pain and suffering of humanity throughout history will be no more. *No longer will there be any curse* (22:3) probably refers to the removal of the dire consequences of the disobedience of God in Genesis 3. The word here used for "tree" (*xylos*) is not the usual word used elsewhere in the New Testament, but a word meaning a dried piece of timber. This is the word used for that "tree" referring to the cross on which Jesus died and by which he healed us (Acts 5:30; 10:39; 13:29; Galatians 3:13; 1 Peter 2:24). This "tree" gives life to all who eat its fruit. Ezekiel 47, the prophecy of the New Temple from which emanates the river that gives life to the whole world, also refers to the endless monthly cycle of the fruiting of the trees and the healing of the leaves. By alluding to the New Temple prophecy in Ezekiel 47, John is teaching yet again that the City of God is a Temple City, a city from which God and the Lamb rule and in which they are worshipped.

A brief description of life in the city now follows (22:3b-5). Three statements are made about the blessings to be enjoyed by the people of the City. First, *his servants (douloi) will serve (latreusousin) him*. It is not clear whether the "his . . . him" refers to God or the Lamb. It could be either or both (cf 14.1). The verb "serve" used here means "worship" and it is taken in that sense by the RSV. The theme of worship rises to prominence yet again. Second, these servants *will see his face*. Nothing will stand between him and them; they are his and he is theirs. Again it is not stated whose face is seen, God's or the Lamb's; possibly it is the face of both. *His name* (God's, the Lamb's, or both names?) will be on the forehead of the people, a mark of God's ownership of them. They belong to God and the Lamb; they shall see the face of God and the Lamb, something which, in the case of God, had not previously occurred (cf Exodus 33:23; John 1:18). Third, these servants *will reign for ever and ever*. Here is a paradox: servants reigning! Their reign, previously referred to as those raised to life after suffering the "first death", was for "a thousand years" (20:5–6). That reign will continue without end in the City of God.

(5) The words of this prophecy (22:6–21)

The Revelation opened by referring to the "words of the prophecy . . . written . . . in a book" (1:3,11). These words recur repeatedly in the final section of the Revelation:

22.7 The words of the prophecy of this book
22.9 The words of this book
22.10 The words of the prophecy of this book
22.18 The words of the prophecy of this book . . . this
      book
22.19 The words of the book of this prophecy . . . this
      book

These references, coming as they do at the beginning and with such emphasis at the end of the Revelation, serve to tie the whole together. Between his prologue and his epilogue John's prophecy/book is to be found.

The book and what was written in it were of great importance to John, as they were to be to his readers:

22.6   *These words are trustworthy and true*, Jesus
          said.
22.7   *Blessed* is the person who *keeps* these words,
          he said.
22.9   *Angels, prophets* and *servants* of God *keep*
          these words, an angel said.
22.10   The book was *not to be sealed; the time is near.*
22.18–19 Grave warning *not to add* to or *take away from*
          the words of this book.

Clearly John sees his book of prophecy as being of absolute importance, to be read and observed in the churches.

John now adds his personal assurance: *I . . . heard and saw these things.* So awesome were they that John's first impulse was to *fall down* and *worship* the angel who spoke to him and who showed him (22:8). In response, however, the angel gives utterance to what is probably the central message of the Revelation. *"You must not do that"*, he said. *"I am a fellow servant with you . . . .Worship God"* (22:9). Not only is worship to be withheld from Caesar, it is also to be withheld from any created being. Worship may be given only to the Lord God Almighty and to the Lamb.

(6) *I am coming soon (22:6–21)*

There is some uncertainty in this final section as to who the speaker is. On the one hand the speaker is the angel who showed John the New Jerusalem (21:9,15,17; 22:1,9). Yet the context makes it very clear that it is Jesus who is addressing John. In some overarching way, Jesus who spoke to John at the very beginning at Patmos, is speaking to him once more, bringing the whole Revelation to its appointed end. What is his final word? Three times he states that he is coming soon.

22:7   Behold, *I am coming soon.* (Blessed is he who keeps the prophecy of this book)

22:10–12 Do not seal this book. The time is near. Behold *I am coming soon*, bringing my reward. I am Alpha and Omega, first and last, beginning and end. I am the root and offspring of David, the bright and morning star.

22:20   Surely *I am coming soon.*

How will John's readers respond to this? Will they choose to remain in the community of the Lamb or will they slip over into that other community, the people who worship the beast and who bear his mark on their forehead? Will they be inside the city, *blessed* and with *[washed]* *robes* and with access to the *tree of life*, the cross of the Lord Jesus? Or will they be on the outside, with *dogs* (= evil men; Psalm 22:16,20), *sorcerers, fornicators, murderers, idolators and those who love and practise falsehood* (22:15), destined for the "fiery lake" with their god, the beast and with his false prophet. The reader must choose between two possible objects of worship: God/the Lamb or the beast; between two communities: the New

Jerusalem or Babylon; between two destinations: the new heavens and the new earth or the fiery lake. An open invitation is offered to *the thirsty* to come and receive *the free gift of the water of life* (22:17b). It is not too late to be received by the Lamb.

The Revelation concludes powerfully, with a series of invocations, *"come"*. *The Spirit* (speaking through John the prophet) and the bride (the people of Jesus) address their Lord. "Come", they plead. They ask that those who hear this message likewise plead with the Lord, "come". Jesus, the witness of these things says to John, in response to the invocations of prophets and people, *"I am coming soon"*. They say, finally, *Amen, come Lord Jesus*. We join them in that prayer.

❖   ❖   ❖   ❖   ❖   ❖   ❖

Revelation leaves us in no doubt: the great end–time battle of God does not lie in the future but in the past. Christ has conquered the twin evils of guilt and death by his own death and resurrection. As a consequence God's kingdom is now a present reality. These are perhaps the most important keys to the mysteries of this book.

John urgently challenged his readers to worship God and the redeemer Lamb, not the pretentious counterpart, the Roman Emperor. Worship was a test of true conviction and loyalty. To worship Caesar as god was to deny Christ as Lord. To worship God Almighty and the Lamb was to deny Caesar. The many expressions of worship in the Revelation affirm that God and the Lamb were the only ones to whom one could trust one's all.

As we live in the world, and as we meet together with fellow believers, our lives are to be characterised by worship. This means that we say 'yes' to God and the Lamb, but 'no' to every false alternative.

It is to Jesus Christ, however, that most attention is directed. God has bestowed the honour of directly ruling history on Jesus, the Son of God. He is "Lion of the tribe of Judah, the root of David". As God's messiah he shares with God the kingdom of the world, and over the nations he is the "ruler of the kings of the earth" (1:5).

Yet this dominion does not depend on his deity (which is undoubted) but on his victory in the end–time battle of God. It is precisely at this point that the Revelation takes us completely by surprise, as we have seen. The victory of God lies in the past. That victory occurred not in a military campaign but in the death of Jesus. The crowning paradox of the gospel is that Jesus is the Lion of Judah, the Christ authorised to exercise his Father's dominion over history, precisely because he is the Lamb who was slain. "The Lion of the tribe of Judah . . . has conquered" (5:5). In this way the Revelation focuses our attention on Jesus' death, resurrection, ascension, rule and return.

The book repeatedly portrays God as mercifully restraining the destructive powers of the evil king. God is not the source of evil. In his mercy he limits the extent of satanic destruction to provide rebellious humanity with the opportunity to repent from the worship of demons and idols, and from their breaking of his commandments (9:20). In the face of this evil, Christians are continually called on to display patience and faithfulness to Jesus. And it is by endurance and faith that believers share in the completed conquest of the Lamb who was slain.

Through Jesus' redemptive death and their fidelity to him, believers exercise his rule over the devil and all his evil forces. These faithful ones rule on earth during their lifetimes, or they rule from Heaven after their death. They share his messianic rule as Lion of the tribe of Judah. This then is the conquest, the triumph of Christian

166

believers as set out in the Book of Revelation. It is the humble triumph of patient faith in the face of deadly opposition, a triumph which will be realised in physical terms only at the end, in the new Jerusalem.

To his people Jesus says, "I am coming soon". Amen, we say. Come Lord Jesus.

QUESTIONS ON REVELATION CHAPTERS 21–22:

1. What are the hopes for a new world for:

   (a) Marxists?

   (b) Humanists?

   (c) the author of Revelation?

2. Why do these chapters use alternating images of a city and a bride?

3. How meaningful would the promises of 21:5–8 have been to John's readers? How meaningful are they now?

4. How does John's vision of the City of God (21:9–21) contrast with his references to Babylon?

5. What does 'worship' mean in Revelation? How does this relate (a) to our own walk with Christ, and (b) our worship services?

6. How is life in the City of God described? How do our lives reflect the active hope that it will be so incredibly good?

7. How fervent is our plea "Come Lord Jesus"? How earnestly do we desire his return, and the salvation of others for his glory?

Appendix: Symbols in Revelation

The colour white, the images of the throne and the crown	= conquest and rule (divine, human, satanic).
Sea beast and harlot	= Roman emperor and his government
Land beast/false prophet	= Roman provincial governors
Seven	= God and eternal perfection
Six	= Satan's claim to divinity
Three and a half years (or forty two months)	= a period within human history which will come to its end – unlike God's eternity
Twelve	= Leaders of the redeemed
Twenty four	= Leaders from old and new covenants
One hundred forty four thousand	= Redeemed from Israel
Ten	= a round figure
one thousand	= a great number or a very long period
lion	= nobility
ox	= strength
eagle	= speed
man	= wisdom
lamb	= helplessness
horn	= power
eye	= knowledge
right hand	= authority

About the author ...

Throughout his ministry Paul Barnett has tried to combine practical pastoral ministry with academic research and lecturing. This has been reflected in the appointments he has held: rector at St Barnabas' Broadway **and** part time lecturer at Moore College, rector at Holy Trinity Adelaide **and** part time lecturer for the Adelaide Bible Institute, Minister at Trinity Chapel Robert Menzies College (where he is Master) **and** part-time university and Moore College lecturer. He attempts to make some contribution to biblical scholarship, but above all to interpret scholarship to the non–technical reader. He has had a long term interest in ministry to universities, having served as chaplain to both the University of Sydney and Macquarie University. He is also Bishop-elect in the Diocese of Sydney.

His interests include music and current affairs and he enjoys tennis, swimming, fishing and the Aussie bush.

Paul is married to Anita; they have four children.